Trevor Fishlock was born in Heref...  his journalistic career a... sixteen. He became a fre... reporter, and joined *The...* roving commission to fi... Wales tick – to cover the... commentary on the backg... His first book, *Wales and...* lively, absorbing and accur... ...life in Wales, at once humorous and thoughtful.

Also by Trevor Fishlock
Wales and the Welsh

Trevor Fishlock

Talking of Wales

PANTHER
GRANADA PUBLISHING
London Toronto Sydney New York

Published by Granada Publishing Limited
in Panther Books 1978

ISBN 0 586 04555 4

First published in Great Britain by
Cassell & Co Ltd 1976
Copyright © Trevor Fishlock 1976
Cartoons copyright © Cassell & Co Ltd 1976

Granada Publishing Limited
Frogmore, St Albans, Herts AL2 2NF
and
3 Upper James Street, London W1R 4BP
1221 Avenue of the Americas, New York, NY 10020, USA
117 York Street, Sydney, NSW 2000, Australia
100 Skyway Avenue, Toronto, Ontario, Canada M9W 3A6
Trio City, Coventry Street, Johannesburg 2001, South Africa
CML Centre, Queen & Wyndham, Auckland 1, New Zealand

Made and printed in Great Britain by
Cox & Wyman Ltd, London, Reading and Fakenham
Set in Intertype Times

Contents

Preface

In a way my business is to be a professional foreigner; or, if you can allow the contradiction in terms, a resident visitor. As Welsh affairs correspondent of *The Times* my task is to provide a running commentary on the developing story of Wales, and to fill in the background, setting events in their context. I have to get close enough to people and events to understand them, while remaining an observer, uncommitted; aiming to be objective and fair, a reporter. Of course, the longer I live in Wales and drive new headings into the rich and sometimes confusing seams of its history, its political and social and economic background, and two-tongued culture, the harder it is to remain a stranger. At the same time, the knowledge and pleasure I derive is increased by the day. It is a matter of trying to strike a balance, of storing and drawing on experience, while trying to remember, each day, what it was like to be new in Wales. Fortunately, my sense of curiosity has not been dulled and there is much more to find out; indeed, it seems at times that the more I learn the less I know; and the cross-currents and eddies in this land of contradictions keep me fascinated, not to say riveted.

I enjoy Wales enormously and much of my working life is spent roaming it. I can feast on the landscape and I sometimes feel that I can quarry stories from the land itself. I am a Cymruphile, but well aware of the country's creaks and blemishes: I spend much time finding out what makes Wales tick and itch, examining the scars and evidence of torment, the warts, the bald patches and the neuroses. Few small countries have been so persistently skinned and probed by writers, but the magic and the enigma endure. And there is always the vein of humour. I went to the funeral of James Griffiths, the elder statesman of the Labour party and first Secretary of State for Wales. I found a large crowd packed into Ammanford for the service and the chapel was full. I had to call at the local bank just before the funeral and the teller asked me: 'What ticket have you got for the service? Stand or enclosure?'

In the preface to my first book, *Wales and the Welsh*, I wrote that 'these are fascinating times to be in Wales'; and I repeat that now. That book did not attempt to be a definitive work about Welsh history and society, nor does this one. Like the first it aims to be a guide, a briefing, an entertainment, a broad, but not comprehensive, look at the country, the people and their mood. The first part is based upon a walk I made from south to north Wales. The book is, in some respects, the pages from a reporter's notebook and reflects the variety, and perhaps the haphazardness, of a reporter's life: when I awake in the morning I can never be certain where I will be that afternoon or that night; but I always hope I will be turning over fresh stones, meeting new situations, or finding new slants on old themes ... somewhere in Wales.

It may be a source of annoyance to sundry bureaucrats that in this book I keep to the names of the thirteen old counties of Wales. In 1974, under local government reorganization, the thirteen counties were fashioned into eight and were given new names. Most of them were not really new because they were ancient names that had been applied to the regions of Wales long ago. However, I retain the thirteen names for several reasons. Being a product of its time, this book reflects the tendency of most people in Wales to cling to the old names out of habit and out of proper reluctance to let well-worn and well-liked things go, just because someone in London decrees it. There is also the fact that the thirteen counties have distinctive social and geographic characteristics, and often political characteristics, too. They are handy groupings for easy reference. You know where you are when you talk of Anglesey or Denbighshire. You can talk of Cardiganshire and Cardis as a distinct entity. You can talk of Pembrokeshire, and people know what you are talking about; for all of these counties have their own history, problems and identity. So I retain the old names mainly in the interests of clarity. It may be, of course, that I am being sentimental and canutish; but, then, I also have a

certain warm spot for the man in north Wales who keeps a
pub and who has, for several years, with the aid of like-
minded customers, been doing his over-the-counter business
in pounds, shillings and pence, has stood fast for bob and
tanner against the conquering p.

I would like to finish this note by making my acknowl-
edgements. Some fragments in this book appeared originally
in *The Times*. I have quoted some snatches of songs from
the *Broadsides* song book, edited by Peter Meazey and
Dennis O'Neill. Mary Griffith, Elan Closs Stephens, Emyr
Daniel and Geraint Talfan Davies read the typescript and
gave me much thoughtful advice; and Gren Jones, of the
South Wales Echo, drew the cartoons. My thanks to all who
have helped, who have revealed so much of Wales to me.

Cardiff
Wales

CHAPTER ONE

A Blistered Eagle

At last I came down from the bleak hills and out of the storm and into the warm brown Cardiganshire pub. The beating rain had soaked all my clothing hours before and the biting wind had made me feel the first cold finger of exposure: I was storing up aches for my old age. I dripped and shivered like a drenched dog in the low doorway and fished in the bilges of my pocket to pull out a pound note, as damp as seaweed. The landlord had divined my need exactly and was already reaching for the whisky bottle. He lifted an eyebrow and I nodded. He lifted it again and I nodded again. He said he would run the pulpy pound note through the mangle ... and the whisky fell, molten, to rekindle my personal hypocaust.

There was a woman sitting there in the bar with a tanned and friendly face and bright robin eyes. We exchanged grumbles about the weather and she said she was a visitor from Australia.

'You've been up in the mountains,' she said. 'Are you a poet?'

I said I was not.

'Then you must have a Francis Chichester thing; you know, going off all alone.'

I said not really.

'But you must like the mountains.'

I said I did.

'Do you like Dylan Thomas?'

I said I did.

'And his cow-mooing fields?'

Yes.

'And the fishingboat-bobbing sea?'

Yes, I said, and the jollyrogered sea, too.

'Ah,' she noted, satisfied. It was as if we were secret agents who had supplied the correct passwords at a dangerous frontier rendezvous.

'I'm a teacher,' she said. 'But it's hard to interest many Australian people in poetry. It's a sunny country and everyone goes in for sport. And it is a dry country, not at all like Wales. That's why I love Wales. It's so . . .'

Damp. I suggested, squeezing the brim of my hat so that rain water ran into the whisky.

'. . . so old and magical and green and full of stories. You can look around and imagine that all those old bards and old warriors are still in the hills. Where are you travelling?'

I told her I was journeying through the mountains, mainly on foot, partly on horseback, from the Rhondda in the south to Caernarfon in the north. Over the roof of Wales.

She looked out of the window as the rain came tamping down.

'You must feel like an eagle,' she concluded.

With blisters, I said.

I had decided to make the journey simply because it seemed to me it would be an interesting thing to do. A reporter must also be an explorer, and I imagined that both frame and brain needed the excursion and exercise. Only a few people have made similar journeys and Wynford Vaughan-Thomas is one of them. I went to him for advice, for no one knows the land of Wales better than he, and he gave me dinner, with side dishes of anecdotes and rhymes, and some claret and some port to fortify my blood against the rigours of the mountain track. He went to a large table, unrolled my maps, and drew me a route through Wales that would avoid the perils of abysses, bogs, bandits and bores.

A few days later I was up early to ride shotgun on the blue Rhondda bus that makes the early morning expedition from Pontypridd to Maerdy, the last hill station of the Rhondda Fach valley, and right on the crumbling edge of Rhondda civilization. I was to step off at Maerdy and head north until I could bathe my feet, symbolically, in the Menai Strait.

I sat facing the bus conductor and two coal miners. They carefully eyed my newly-dubbined boots, thick Norwegian stockings, fashionably pre-faded denims, sweater and small purposeful rucksack. They said nothing for a while as the bus growled and shook and inched hand-over-hand up one of the Rhondda's junior Eigers.

The conductor's curiosity was the first to crack.

'Duke of Edinburgh's Award?' he tried.

I shook my head and gave a brief outline of my aims. The conductor was unimpressed.

'You'll break your leg up in those hills,' he promised.

One of the miners said: 'It'll be a race who gets to you first – the helicopter or the crows.'

The other miner was more encouraging. 'At least you'll be walking on top of the hills. We'll be digging in the dark a mile below with dust for our dinner. I know what I'd rather be doing any day. When you get to the north have a pee in the sea for me.'

The damp slates and pavements were getting a gleam on them as the sun began to clock in. Women were shaking out mats, and pale-faced men were emerging from their doors with their snap-tins, vacuum flasks and *Daily Mirrors* and *Western Mails*, coughing and lighting small cigarettes to flush the fresh morning air from their lungs.

Some people hate the Rhondda. They hate it for its past, or its present, or both. Or for its appearance. It is no Eden, that's for certain, but I find it rugged, stubborn and grand; I like it for its own sake and I have no inclination to follow the platoons of sociologists and other official pulse-takers who, over the years, have seen Rhondda only as a patient, an interesting case-study. I look at Rhondda as I look at any other interesting part of Wales. I am enthralled by its atmosphere of history and struggle and perhaps that is a luxury because I have never lived there. Of course, its unique ant-hill culture has almost vanished now and all but two of the pits have closed in what was once the mightiest and most intensively mined coal district of the world. Cars used to get punctured tyres through running over studs that fell from miners' boots, but today there are far more cars than miners. There are half-dead cells of bingo where once there were libraries; and those libraries in the Rhondda and other valleys were, perhaps, the finest working-class libraries in Britain. They fired imaginations and aided escape; they fuelled the minds of a race of remarkable men of influence: miners' leaders, politicians, scholars, musicians. Now most of the books have been cleared out, sometimes sold for a song to make way for television lounges, bars and guitars. And along with men who learned their way out went men who fought their way out with fists and footwork, the punchmen who drew crowds to Judges Hall and Llwynypia Baths, the heroes like Boyo Rees, Llew Edwards, Jimmy Wilde and Tommy Farr, the Tylorstown Terror, who brought excitement and glamour to the valleys and whose faded sepia photographs, in noble stance, still adorn walls in pubs.

But some people will be growing impatient with all this talk of Rhondda. They will be muttering, with some justification, that people seem to think that the Rhondda is the only valley in south Wales, that it seems to get all the attention of visiting writers and cameramen. It is true that many people who do not know Wales have a vague notion that the Rhondda extends roughly from the racecourse at Chepstow to Merlin's oak in Carmarthen; indeed, that it is all of south Wales. In reality though the Rhondda is only part of the story, and it is not possible to know Wales without knowing something of the turbulent history of the whole region of mining valleys. There are twenty-two main valleys in Glamorgan, Monmouthshire and Carmarthenshire, and their names are impressed in heavy type in the story of Wales: Gwendraeth – Fach and Fawr – Amman, Dulais, Swansea, Neath, Llynfi, Garw, Ogwr, Gilfach, Rhondda Fawr and Rhondda Fach, Ynysybwl, Cynon, Merthyr, Taff, Bedlinog, Rhymney, Sirhowy, Ebbw Fawr and Ebbw Fach, and Llwyi. In some respects they are all much the same, the blighted chines of coal and steel. In other respects, each is different and the inhabitants identify strongly with their native valley, feeling that their own community is a little different from, and a little better than, the one next door.

'Don't go to the Rhondda,' an industrialist said to me when I first arrived in south Wales and talked to him about my plans to write an article about local economic problems. 'All the journalists and film crews go up there. The

Rhondda has become a cliché. Go to the valley I come from.
It's much better. Anyway, they are all big-heads up in the
Rhondda. They think they own Wales.'

The valleys were the birthplace and nursery of the industrial revolution in Britain and because of their coal and iron
and steel were the prime generator of British economic
growth. They were a social and political storm centre, a cru-
cible of suffering and change. They were also a melting pot –
the Rhondda especially – of Englishmen, Irishmen, Scots,
Italians, Germans, Greeks, Portuguese who came to join
with Welshmen in the search for work and the creation of a
vivacious and unusual society – not primarily Celtic, like
many other parts of Wales, but certainly very Welsh. A lot
of the stuffing has been knocked out of the valleys because
of the decline in the number of south Wales pits to forty-
eight, and the long programme of modernization in the steel
industry which has made many men redundant. The valleys
no longer teem and throb as they did years ago, but they still
provide a high quality of community life, and a way of living
balanced between town and country, that is valued by the
people.

'I've travelled the world and I've lived in parts of England
– but Ebbw Vale is the place for me. It's where I was born
and bred and it's where I want to raise my kids,' an ex-
steelworker said. He had just been made redundant from the
Ebbw Vale steel plant and was on a government training
course, training to be a machine tool fitter. 'I want to get
a job nearby so that I can go on living in the valley. It's a
friendly community and it's the only place where I feel really
comfortable.'

Recently, many of the valleys people have been taking
stock of their situation: their region is, after all, the home of
perhaps seven hundred thousand, and, with better roads and
social services as well as more industrial settlement, the
valleys could have a decent future, holding prospects for the
young men and women. In some valleys depopulation has
been halted because young people find it easier to stay put
and buy a house locally than head for the large towns and
cities where house prices are too high for them. The aban-
doning of a plan to build a new town at Llantrisant, a few

miles below the Rhondda, seemed to many valleys people a
sensible and positive decision, an encouragement for local
authorities to get on more quickly with the work of renewal.
During 1974 and 1975 an effort was made to stimulate
valleys people to look closely, perhaps for the first time, at
their history and uncertain future. It consisted of a series of
conferences and community and educational projects and
grew, essentially, from the experience of Aberfan. The after-
math of the disaster here was not all wretched. There
emerged qualities of leadership, loyalty and strength. The
community might easily have been torn apart, but only a
handful of people left it and a basic unity was forged. The
heart of Aberfan, once the initial shock had subsided, has
been its inhabitants' belief in their community and their own
strength. And some people feel that Aberfan's experience of
finding leaders from its own ranks, when they were most
needed, and of discovering an unsuspected community
power, provides a lesson for other towns and villages in
south Wales where leadership is needed.

Yet depopulation and a certain apathy remain a part of
the core of the valleys' difficulties. At a public meeting in the
Rhondda, a local councillor made an unconscious and
moving comment on the modern valleys when, in the
fashion of the times, he chastised the commercial television
company for replacing an American melodrama series with
a Welsh programme. 'Bring back,' he cried, 'bring back *The
Human Jungle* to the Rhondda!'

The bus stopped about three-quarters of the way up the
valley and the conductor took the opportunity to jump off
and wave his arms furiously at a couple of sheep rooting
about in a dustbin on the pavement.

'Gerroutovit!' he shouted.

They gorroutovit, sloping off reluctantly with shifty side-
long Humphrey Bogart looks. Valley sheep are not like the
white and woolly ninepence-to-the-shilling dumplings of
nursery books and popular imagination. They are public
enemy number one, with tattered grey fleeces and insolent
baas, biting the babies and butting the wives. In south Wales
the gardeners await the invention of an aerosol spray that

will knock out both greenfly and sheep: strong men have wept to see their gardens roughed-up and their dahlias chewed. In response to the public mutterings about sheep atrocities the Welsh Office has established a special department to find ways of bringing the beasts under control. Some districts have sheep pounds and employ wardens, the fleece police, to round up strays. And farmers in one valley have been warned that if not claimed quickly their impounded animals will be cut up and fed to the local old-age pensioners.

There are more than six million sheep in Wales and I felt that I met most of them during my journey. They pouted like peeved princesses as I stomped by. Their numbers increase while, in the hills, the human population declines. They are one of the constants, like legends and rain, and, somehow, sheep always seem to get in on the act in Wales.

One morning, in a street in one of the thin valleys of the south, a sheep fainted. Who can say why sheep swoon? Perhaps their fleeces grow too heavy to bear, perhaps sudden excitements are too much for them. In this case, whatever the reason, the beast emitted a croak, flopped senseless and rolled against the front door of one of the grey stone terraced houses.

Hearing the thud, the owner-occupier broke off from shaving and went to the door. He looked down at the shuddering and unconscious sheep and then up the street as a trio of his workmates approached.

'What's up, Dai?' they called.

'This sheep's fainted.'

It was enough. In a land where the cult of the nickname is strongly rooted, it was enough. From that day to this the man has been known in his locality as Dai Sheep Fainting. Naturally, in a society where people share relatively few surnames, like Jones, Evans, Williams, Thomas, Davies and the like, nicknames have been a necessity for purposes of identification. But they also developed into a humorous art form, now dying out, in which an individual's appearance, a deformity or a quirk of speech or habit was encapsulated in a word or two. Thus Maldwyn Etcetera and Dai-let-me-see were named after phrases they used often. Tom Iron Belly could eat anything; Tommy One Tune was the most boring cinema organist in south Wales; Dai Drop had been a para-trooper; Evans Fifty Ribs had several narrow escapes underground and each time he was dug out he would say: 'I'm all right, boys, only a few ribs broken.' Jones Whodunit was an inveterate reader of detective stories; the staff re-porter of the Press Association in Wales is seen so often in telephone boxes dictating his reports to London that he is known throughout Welsh journalism as Cliff Kiosk. A water diviner is known as Thomas the Twig, on account of his trembling hazel. An undertaker near Swansea is known as Dai Box. A baker in west Wales was known locally as Jones the Crust – until the Queen visited his village and stopped to chat with him; now he is known as Jones Upper Crust. In the pits the nicknames have often been of an earthy kind. Rees Buggerhell was named after his favourite oath, and Davies Cough-and-spit and Billy Firing Fart after their somewhat unfortunate habits.

I left the bus in Maerdy square with the conductor look-ing at me as if he expected to read about me in the evening paper before the week was out. The paths in the hills and valleys of this region have been fairly well trodden by travel-lers and writers, particularly in the nineteenth century, and as part of my research before setting out, I re-read Marie Tre-velyan's account of life in this area which she wrote in 1892. In the style of her time, she wrote of the native people in the same way that her pith-helmeted contemporaries wrote of pygmies and fuzzywuzzies.

'The hill women,' she noted, 'are fond of drinking tea in immoderate quantities and that is why their complexions fade early and leave a sallow and muddy colour upon the skin . . . the teapot is always on the hob and there is no end to the potations. To many people the hill folk appear to be only rough, uncouth and coarse specimens of humanity, very necessary as workers in iron, or toilers in darksome pits, as beasts of burden and brainless adjuncts to machinery. The thoughtful mind sees in these people many good qualities of head and heart. Their characteristics are patient plodding and indomitable perseverance. They may be slow to receive, or to work out, an idea, but they are above all things sure, and quite willing to take helpful suggestions. For industry they closely resemble the Germans, and perhaps in slight tendencies to obstinacy they are also allied to the same people. Their brains are strong, and so far as I have been able to learn, there is but little insanity among the hill population.'

Writers in that pre-magnetic-tape age tried to put more colour into their work by attempting reproductions of what they thought was Welsh speech. Marie Trevelyan sprinkled phrases like indeed-to-goodness here and there, and gave this account of a country couple visiting the Swansea *eisteddfod*:

'He-er's-a-greet-town.'

'Yess-inteet-an-it-iss-very-goot-to-be-he-er.'

'Give-uss-two-basins-of-leek-proth.'

'Weeth-a-bit-of-bread-an'-sheese.'

She added that 'these glimpses from real life serve to illustrate the primitive character of the Welsh'. Reading accounts like this makes one feel that Victorian writers hunted the Welsh with bait and weighted nets as well as pens and notebooks; and sometimes I think that attitudes to Wales have not changed much in eighty years.

I plodded past Maerdy colliery and watched the wheel spinning and imagined the men far below. Maerdy has some narrow and awkward seams and working conditions are harder than in many pits. Sometimes politicians who have asked to see a coal mine are taken down Maerdy pit, and the experience is usually reckoned to be especially educating for them. For anyone who normally goes to work in a collar and tie, or in neat overalls, a journey into a mine is a salutary experience. At the coalface the whine and clatter of machinery, the dust glinting in the light of the helmet lamp, the cramped conditions, the awareness of danger, combine to give a stark insight into the miner's life. A coalface has all the noise, activity and discomfort of a gundeck on a wooden-waller in action.

Once you have drawn your lamp from the lamp room and entered the cage that descends the shaft at thirty feet a

second, miners freely admit you to their unique com-
radeship. They have a strong sense of loyalty to the particular pit they are working in, but they cling much more
strongly to themselves, to their working way of life and the
mates that are part of it. Theirs is a manly trade and they
take pride in their craftsmanship, their ruggedness, their acceptance of risks. They are watchful and aware of their sur-
roundings and their humour is sharp and dry. At the bottom
of Marine colliery near Ebbw Vale, a miner pointed out to
me a piece of timber, about seven feet long, on which a man
had chalked a message to his mate. 'Sam – I've got your
stuff,' it read. 'PS (Security) when you've read this message,
eat it.' The journey to the coal-face was about a mile and a
half and we often stooped under the low roof. A pit is no
place for a claustrophobe and some miners say that a pit is
no place for man or beast. But at least, touch wood, the
miners have a good chance of coming up at the end of their
daily shifts, unlike that special class of colliery worker, the
pit pony. Apart from an annual three weeks' holiday in the
summer these animals stay down the pit. But it is not so
bad as it sounds. A pit pony is not really a pony at all,
he stands thirteen to fifteen hands, has the build of a junior
carthorse and enjoys the official and more dignified title
of colliery horse. He is highly regarded, and guarded by
rules and attention that befits his special status. All the
colliery horses are geldings selected for steady temperament
and have to be at least four years old before going underground. At pit bottom they live in well-lit and well-venti-
lated stables, feeding on chaff and crushed oats from the
Coal Board's central granary in Ebbw Vale. They work a
forty-eight hour week and, contrary to popularly held
belief, are not blind. 'What,' a miner demanded, 'would be
the use of a blind horse?' Because they are handsomely
treated and because the atmosphere in a pit is virtually ster-
ile, the horses tend not to get the illnesses that afflict
animals on the surface; and they do not contract pneu-
moconiosis, the dust disease that silts the lungs of miners
and leaves thousands of men breathless and crippled when
they should be enjoying their mature years. There is no fixed
retirement age for colliery horses, but the ostler and the vet

usually pension them off somewhere between fifteen and twenty, and all of them go to selected retirement homes. It is surprising, really, that in a highly mechanized business like coal mining there should still be room for horses. After the Second World War there were more than five thousand horses working in Welsh pits and today there are about eighty. They don't haul coal, but they provide power and transport in the parts of mines where machinery cannot go, or where it would be too expensive to take machines. Thus they transport supplies and salvage material and carry the gear which is needed to maintain air passages. They are economical and efficient. The bond between miners and colliery horses is renowned in the coalfields, and the stories of equine heroism, faithfulness and cussedness are legion. No mining community is without its tale of miners being led to safety through damaged pitch-black tunnels by hanging on to their horses' tails; or of horses saving lives by stopping in their tracks and refusing to budge – just before a roof fall. One wonder horse is said to have braced its body against a bulging and collapsing wall while miners scrambled past to safety. Once, in the days before nationalization of the mining industry, a horse dropped dead in a mine owned by a hated employer. A miner pencilled a note and stuck it between the beast's teeth.

'Boss,' it said, 'I would rather die than work for you.'

I spent several hours underground at Marine colliery and had to return to the surface because I was anxious to keep an interview appointment with Sir Julian Hodge, the millionaire banker. There was no time to bath, so I washed my hands and face quickly and put on a shirt, the collar just covering the tide mark and dashed off to Cardiff. I was just in time to be only a little late for the appointment. A few hours earlier the steel pit cage had taken me four hundred yards beneath the ground – miners measure shafts in yards, not feet – and now I was in the panelled lift of the Hodge building being whisked to the fourteenth floor to see a king in his counting house. When I had left the pit there were some miners at the pit head soaping and washing, and now Sir Julian emerged to meet me, his cuffs drawn back and soap on his hands. He talked about his plans for the new

Commercial Bank of Wales which were then coming to fruition. He said his dream of founding the bank, a bank to aid development in Wales, was seeded when he was given a note from the old Bank of Newport, dated 1812. He reminisced for a while on his days as a railway clerk when he studied accountancy and took the first steps towards becoming a financier on a large scale. 'Luck is an indispensable ingredient of success and when I look back, I have to pinch myself to believe it all.' He crossed the soft carpet to show me his collection of old banknotes, of which he is proud, neatly arrayed in plastic albums. From this hushed and sanitized fourteenth-floor suite the bottom of the pit, and the men working there in din and darkness, seemed to be the far side of the moon.

It was a cool day in May, with the rain pecking a little, a dabbledy day as they say in Herefordshire, and some squalls whooshed across the rough moor grass like the slipstream of Guto Nyth Bran, the fastest thing on feet, who, in the eighteenth century, ran some astonishing races in the hills and valleys of south Wales. He is recorded as having once run twelve miles in fifty-three minutes and he would have made a snail of Wilson, the wonder athlete, who featured in one of my boyhood comics. The track now went past the Lluest Wen reservoir and as I climbed higher up Mynydd Bwllfa the Rhondda dropped away, the sun broke through and the humped shoulders of the Brecon Beacons rose up suddenly, like theatre scenery, on my right.

There is nothing quite like walking the high ground of Wales, and nothing quite like sitting on the milestone to master the view.

It is a good way of taking stock as well as air. Out of the wind there is the silence of the high places and the grandeur of mountains unrolling; the hiss of the breeze in rocks and spiky grass; the faint bleat of sheep, random specks high above and far below; a whiff of woodsmoke from small farmhouses; dashing adolescent river, sunshine on pools; bleached skulls of sheep, and crows pecking bones; a glimpse of a fox washing his face, a startled hare, jet-propelled; swinging buzzards, and a sight of the rare red kite.

There are roofless broken cottages in valleys in the interior, from which men retreated long ago; decayed chapels, once heaven's hill forts, now pewless and dank after the exodus. The rusting machinery of the metal miners, their wagons, pumps and winches, lies abandoned like the cutlery on the *Mary Celeste*. There is the splendid violence of bad weather and the feel of hostility as early darkness closes in and mist and rain bully you down from the hills.

The wild Wales described by nineteenth-century travellers and painters is still there all right; smaller, beleaguered, but surviving. I walked in some of the finest mountain country anywhere in the world and, in the country, heard more Welsh spoken than English. There is still wilderness and its antiquity and beauty remain endlessly impressive. It seems unchanging, but of course it is changing, and not always subtly and for the better. In a few years it will not be possible for you to see all that I saw, for in the upland districts many of the great mountain haunches are being draped with huge antimacassars of coniferous duffle. A large part of the beauty of the high land is its nakedness; so if you want to see it hurry while stocks last.

It would be easy and right in fashion to toll a bell for life in rural Wales. It is true that the path to England and its big cities is still beaten by many of the young, and especially the natural leaders, the gifted and the business-minded. The cities of England number among their inhabitants many thousands of émigrés who are Welsh by origin and English, by pay-packet, and many of them would some day, somehow, like to go back; but by the time they have got their money they have forgotten their language. It is true that the Welsh language, which is strongly rooted in the countryside, is being eroded to an extent which makes many people angry or despairing. It is true that the making of a living in the country will always be difficult, and sometimes hard – whatever the romantics say. And yet wild Wales has a chance. In small numbers, people are moving in and moving back. Some are drifters but many settle. Small industries are being started and although some fail most are building and growing. Inch by inch small dams are being built against depopulation. It is a race against time. It may be lost. But there is a widening appreciation that life in the country can be better and that if the right effort is made it can be worthwhile socially and culturally and economically.

Somehow Wales itself retains its identity and patches up the damage to it. The survival of this small country, against all the odds, is astonishing. The values and facets of its life that make it different from England, that make it unique, are chipped and battered – but still the words Wales and Welsh have significant meanings. For centuries Wales has been at the very core of the British empire and Welshmen, like Scots, did at least their share towards building and maintaining it, sinking their own talents and identities into the great British adventure. Yet, after the great oak had sprouted, grown to maturity, flourished and, at last, withered, Wales was left – not the same, of course – but with the essence of its personality intact; and that is remarkable. The Welsh have remained to Englishmen a rather baffling breed, and bits of Wales and the Welsh are still an unravelled enigma, even to the Welsh themselves.

The past few years have been a time of great change in Wales. In my own short experience, seven years of reporting Welsh affairs, I have written not only about the changing pattern of politics, industry and employment, the economic and cultural developments, but also about the changing attitudes of the people and, in particular, the revision of attitudes towards their own identity and their place in the present.

For me, one of the more striking developments is a growth of self-confidence; a willingness of the Welsh to be themselves. It is only now, in the last quarter of the twentieth century, that the bulk of Welsh people feel able to regard themselves as absolute equals with Englishmen, to squash the old and imposed inferiority and to stop apologizing for being Welsh. It has taken a long time and the cure is by no means complete and universal. But it is progressing steadily.

A hundred and twenty years ago the people of Wales had little to sustain their national life or, indeed, much of a concept of themselves as an entity. They had none of the institutions so important for a country's self-respect: no university, no popular storehouse and seedbed for their culture, no national museum or national library, no effective way of guarding their language. They were exploited on the land and in the pits and represented in Parliament by Tory landowners who were regarded as aliens. The language through which the ordinary people expressed themselves was scorned by the small middle class and the authorities. The government, through the education authorities, and with the ready co-operation of the Welsh people themselves, was soon to embark on a programme that was intended to wipe the language out and bind the Welsh more closely to England under the mighty aegis of English. As it happened, the Welsh language was a tougher nut than anyone appreciated. The education system that developed in the nineteenth century had not much room for Welsh history and this century, too, only a minority of the people have been taught something of their own history because the system has concentrated overwhelmingly, and in many parts exclusively, on English people. In a sense the Welsh have been a stranded people.

In England, the received idea of the Welsh has usually been that of a crowd of people who were folksy and quaint, mentally incomplete sometimes, and sometimes sharply devious; a little savage, probably dirty, somewhat servile and with a comic way of speaking English. The Welsh, in popular imagination east of the dyke, were basically two-legged pit ponies who could sing, and you had to keep an eye on them or they would twist you or stir up trouble; being Celts, they were emotional and sentimental and lacked that good old English quality, steadiness. This image of the Welsh was reinforced by writers. I have already referred to the reproductions of 'funny' Welsh speech. Newspapers, magazines and music-hall comedians fed the image and Welshmen, encouraged at all times to take Englishness to their bosoms, came to believe that the English view of them was an accurate one. It was inevitable that a book like *The Perfidious Welshman*, written by an Alf Garnett figure who skulked beneath a pseudonym, should appear in the early years of this century: it was a remorseless attack on the

Welsh people, supposedly a humorous work, but a remarkable indication of the contempt in which the Welsh were
held. 'Anglicize yourself,' the author told Welshmen, 'as
speedily as you can. It will never be possible for you to be
equal to an Englishman, but you may make him your
ideal and you may realize the misfortune of having been
born Welsh. Forget your language as quickly as you can.
It is vulgar to use it in decent society. Never mention
your own country or its "history" more often than you can
help.'

To Englishmen, the author gave this advice: 'Never allow
your children to be contaminated by the manners of Welsh
children. Avoid the Welsh language as you would sin. Do
not have a Welsh servant who is walking out with a young
man. She can seldom be doing that and remain pure.
Cautious Taffy satisfies himself that the lady of his choice
will become a mother before the marriage takes place. Never
employ a Welshman if you can help it, for he will not only be
dishonest but he will slander you all over the countryside . . .
His Majesty King Edward VII will endure anything for the
sake of his people. He will listen to niggers' tom-toms and
suffer a Cymric choir to bellow and shriek at him . . . Taffy is
a low-bred mongrel of Mongolian origin. The casual observer cannot have failed to notice the distinctive traces of
this racial origin. Not only have we the Welshman's dialect,
which is obviously a blend of Semitic and other tongues, but
the cast of features, inferior intellect, excitability, de-
ceitfulness and absurd vanity all seem to prove that Taffy is,
for the most part, a remnant of the Mongolian race . . .'

And so on, and so on, in tedious diatribe. The snickering
over the Welsh language went hand-in-hand with official
prejudice. The authorities, aided and abetted by some of the
Welsh people themselves, worked to rid Wales of the
language. It is reasonable to conclude that antipathy to
Welsh on the part of the authorities played a considerable
part in the sense of inferiority that was for many years a
characteristic of the Welsh people and the traces of it have
not yet been holystoned away. A language is a lot more than
an arrangement of ciphers and sounds to communicate information and when you place a people's language in a

second-class category you place the people themselves in it, too.

The national movement that has developed in Wales in the past ten years or so is not the burgeoning of a brand-new phenomenon. It is essentially the strengthening of a current that has existed in Wales for a long time. The national movement has been a movement for self-confidence, a slow struggle to create a framework within which the Welsh can express themselves freely, a framework within which they may be themselves, keep the things that are theirs and take a strong part in the management of their country. That, basically, is what modern Welsh nationalism is about. The national movement, both political and apolitical, has been much broader than the critics of Welsh aspirations and political nationalism realize – and the achievements of the national movement have been considerable. Perhaps it ought to be said that nationalism is not the exclusive property of the Welsh Nationalist party: it exists, sometimes shy and unacknowledged, across the political spectrum. From the small beginning of a cultural renaissance in the eighteenth and nineteenth centuries, when scholars, poets and gents of leisure interested themselves in collecting manuscripts and promoting exploration of Welsh literature, Welshmen started to build. They had very little to start from – the awareness of Welshness had been dormant for centuries – and the journey was an uphill one. Since that time, almost every achievement of the Welsh movement has been in the face of criticism, and dogged by doubt and the fog-bank of apathy.

But the university was built, the *eisteddfod* established as a substantial festival, the library and museum were founded. The chapels created a system for education, debate and democracy and the encouragement of Welsh. There developed a movement to stiffen the framework of Welshness with political and administrative girders. Political nationalism itself has been a tidal force, but, slowly, Welshmen won for themselves the machinery they wanted to help them play a greater part in governing their own country. To a network of cultural, educational and economic advisory bodies they added a department of state, the Welsh Office, and a seat in the British cabinet. They also began to build a broadcasting service for Wales and for the Welsh language and to push for an elected assembly to manage their affairs. They founded a Welsh Trades Union Congress. The devolution of power and administration from London, over a broad range of activities, had become respectable and realistic. Thus the Welsh, during the 1960s and 1970s, began to feel themselves less of a province and more of a people.

What Welshmen sought for many years was equality with their English neighbours, and they imagined that they would achieve it through universal fluency in the English language. It was important and necessary that they should possess English – it provided new vistas, new skills, a major economic and cultural key – and Welsh parents during the past century have needed no extra persuasion on this point. But linguistic equality is not everything. Welshmen thought that Welsh was an obstacle in the path of progress; they thought they could have either English or Welsh and that they would have to throw the old language over the side. They were mistaken. Only a minority saw that they could have both. Linguistic equality and greater integration with England have not meant that Wales has been better governed or less neglected: any brief reading of the economic history of Wales bears witness to that. If Welshmen and English administrators hoped that linguistic equality would batten down the hatches on the concept of Welsh identity and nationhood, they were mistaken. People have found it relatively easy to shrug off Welsh, but hard to shrug off Wales – and that is partly because the language is so ingrained. I believe it is important, when looking at modern Wales, to consider the achievements of the national movement during the past century, to take the broad view. It is unprofitable to bewail the small set-backs in the progress towards self-confidence – which is the progress towards genuine equality.

Wales today is a healthier and better country than it has ever been. It is true that the language is going through its largest crisis, that there is a race against time to stabilize it. It is true that there is still a distressing element of servility among some Welsh people. It is true that introspection is something of a hobby with many; but then, I suppose, Wales has a very interesting navel to contemplate. On the other hand, many more people have the awareness that confidence brings and they do not have the old hallmark of Welshness: the congenital stiff neck brought about by years of looking over their shoulders to see if the English approved of what they were doing. I hear and read the phrase 'What on earth will the English think of us?' less today than I did six or seven years ago. I think more people are prepared to acknowledge their Welshness unselfconsciously, where their fathers might have preferred to be secretive about it. I find — a small point, but interesting — that many Welshmen now write 'Welsh' or 'Cymro' in the nationality column of hotel registers, rather than 'British'. I believe that far more Welshmen today look at certain economic, social and political questions with a regard for the benefits and disadvantages to Wales, rather than Britain. There are some Welshmen who think of their part of the world as a big English county, like Yorkshire; or even two counties; but there are far more who regard Wales as an entity and a country and as something rather more than a sub-region rather good at rugby.

Some of the changes in Welsh life, and in the outlook of Welsh people, may come as a surprise to those Englishmen whose knowledge of Wales is scanty and founded in ill-taught history and in myths and jokes.

The cap-touching crew of Taffs, the butts of stage, screen and novels, who emerged blinking from underground toil to slot their hips into fireside zinc tubs before heading for choir practice, or the stirring of industrial trouble, or a homily on the demon alcohol from their nearest nonconformist sentry-box, may have existed once. But no longer. Times have changed and Wales is not a backwater. The changes and the complex currents make it a stimulating country. Not everyone agrees, I know; least of all the exiled Englishman who wrote this touching letter to a pop music magazine:

'Wales is incredibly boring and miles behind everywhere else in the world. If there weren't such good pop groups from Wales like Man and Good Habit, I'd have shot myself years ago.'

In stating that the clichés are not the whole truth, I am not claiming that the facets of Wales best known to people out-side are fictional. Let us consider the question of Wales, the land of song. This particular image developed during the nineteenth century when there were large choirs, set-piece choir battles and marathon singing sessions.

('Wales?' a taxi driver in New York said, screwing up his face. 'Whales? Wales? D'you mean da fish or them singing bastards?')

Music in Wales today has broken out of the narrow confines of the choral tradition. And because the choirs are more sophisticated and versatile there is a sense in which Wales is now more of a musical nation than it ever was. But singing remains an important means of informal expression and enjoyment, and older people, in particular, like to draw upon the hymns and anthems of their youth and childhood for their mutual entertainment. It so happens that this kind of singing often blooms best fairly late in the evening, and I speak as one who has thrilled to the sound of the baritones drowning the barman's helpless and repeated cries of 'Last orders, please!' On several occasions I have learned the real meaning of *Ar hyd y nos** and have heard the crowing of the cock persuade the tenors and basses to put their voice-boxes to bed at last. Yes, the Welsh sing all right. They can dig deeply into seams of memory and cultural experience for their tunes and harmonies. Certainly they are expected to sing, to live out the cliché, and, pound for pound, they prob-ably sing more, and better, than other nations.

The chapels are another part of the familiar picture of Wales. They are still a force, but a depleted one. Their influence is still a part of the background of many of the people, and in many districts of rural Wales they remain a focus of community life. But a lot of chapels are empty and have broken windows and holed roofs, as if they have been shelled. Some have been bought up by bright young men and converted into modern machines for living and there is colour television where the pulpit used to be. Preachers today are not so athletic as they were in the old days, and some veteran chapel-goers hanker for the era of brimstone sermons and the *hwyl* preachers who used the pulpit like a

* All through the night.

boxing ring as they fought to get the devil on the ropes. As
the chapels have declined, so has the temperance movement,
and the areas where there is still Sunday closing of pubs
grow fewer. The Sabbath-shuttered pub became part of the
Welsh scene under the Sunday Closing Act of 1880, when
chapel rule was powerful and people flocked to sign the
pledge of abstinence. The quiet Sunday, the Welsh Sunday,
unstained by alcohol, was once a mighty institution, and
Wales was an almost teetotalitarian state for one day a week.
A friend of mine recalls that as a lad of fourteen he made his
first appearance on a public stage giving a talk entitled 'The
Menace of Medicated Wine'. And mothers who gave their
babies gripe water were condemned for giving the mites a
taste for liquor.

But, of course, men still wanted a drink on Sundays and,
particularly after the Second World War, the gap was filled
by clubs, much to the annoyance of those licensees who
wanted to open and saw some of their trade being drained
away from them. Some inns did open to their regular customers – and the history of clandestine Sunday drinking,
rich in a folklore of skulking and subterfuge, has still to be
written. There was a publican who laid a garden hose from
his best-bitter pump to the front room of a neighbouring
house. There was a policeman, a member of a regular coterie
of Sunday drinkers, who was ordered to take part in a raid on
his own pub one Sunday morning. He wrote down the names
and gave evidence, but the guilty men said not a word to in-
criminate him. Such was the loyalty of the undercover drinker.
Once, when police raided a riverside pub, two customers
dived out of the back door and into a small boat, giving a
fair impression of Henley Regatta as they rowed to safety.

Meanwhile, in Sunday-open pubs just across the English
border, the Saxon hosts tapped their casks and rehearsed
their smiling *bore da*'s as they readied to meet the Celtic
hordes. In 1961, however, the law was amended and the
people of Wales were allowed to settle the matter among
themselves by having a referendum every seven years. In the
first poll the four boroughs of Cardiff, Newport, Swansea and
Merthyr Tydfil, along with Breconshire, Radnorshire, Flintshire, Glamorgan and Monmouthshire, voted to open on

Sundays. In the next poll they were joined by Pembrokeshire, Montgomeryshire and Denbighshire. That poll put an
end to the bizarre situation at one inn which straddled the
wet-dry border: on Sundays the public bar had been dry and
empty, but the lounge bar was wet and crowded. The
Sunday-opening lobby hoped that in the third referendum in
November 1975 all Wales would embrace the brewer. But
they were disappointed. Certainly some more pub doors
were unbolted on the margins, bringing a Sunday pint within
reach of nine-tenths of the people of Wales, but the tradition
of the Welsh Sunday endured. The fastnesses of Welsh
Wales retained the dry Sunday and those who wanted a
drink and the talk that went with it had to join a club or
walk or drive across the boundary. Those with a taste for a
lightweight Sunday adventure, as well as a need for an aperi-
tif, could go for a ride in the little red wood-panelled buffet
car of the Ffestiniog narrow-gauge railway, a thin wet line in
Sunday-dry Caernarfonshire. Today, the temperance movement fights on, a rearguard action now, but just as determined. Recently, a minister who failed to stop a club
adjacent to his chapel opening on a Sunday morning, at least
shamed the club management into cancelling the booking of
a strip-tease dancer. Drinking on a Sunday is one thing;
drinking within earshot of people at prayer is at least a tolerable situation. But watching a girl show you her bottom at
the same time, and before lunch, too – the decadence and
incongruity of it reached even the most sodden.

The chapel age gave the Welsh an undeserved reputation
for gloominess and pinched features; and I suppose the
annual competition for Best Kept Graveyard in Radnorshire – you can see the plaque awarded as a prize as you
drive through the county – fits the image. Some funerals,
however, were, and are, public affairs, in the Celtic tradition,
with food and drink around the coffin, not unenjoyable if a
good old man had died, well loved after a useful life; and
sometimes had a black humour about them. In Monmouthshire some years ago a group of old men, entrusted
with the task of burying their friend in the hillside graveyard, found they had forgotten the ropes to lower the coffin
into the grave. Emboldened by the drink he had taken be-

forehand, one of them jumped into the grave and shouted to the others to manhandle the coffin down while he gave support from below. Just before they let go they realized that there would be no way of retrieving the man, so they hauled him out, and, with a shout of 'Drop it gently, boys!' allowed the coffin to fall into the grave with a great thud. In the same valley a member of the Home Guard died and the community had its first military funeral of the war. One of the comrades-in-arms stood stiffly to attention as Last Post was played; he was resplendent in khaki battledress topped by – the traditional funeral headgear – a bowler hat. There was a chapel deacon in Monmouthshire who was devastated by the passing of his black cat. In an attempt to provide some kind of a life after death, he had the creature skinned and made into a sleek binding for his Bible. The tail, still attached, was used as a page-marker.

The Welsh and drink, the Welsh and death, are fields that have interested commentators from time to time. But what of the Welsh and sex? This is a field that requires the most delicate investigatory technique. I have never been so blunt as a curious Englishman who asked an acquaintance of mine: 'Do people actually, I mean, do they really , er, m**e l*ve, in Welsh?' He was assured that they do, except when they make it in silence.

'The Welsh,' an Englishman who has lived in Wales for several years said to me, 'are hypocrites. Supposing a Welshman has a daughter of nineteen and a son of eighteen and they both arrive home one evening, the son the worse for drink and the daughter confessing that she is to have a child without benefit of clergy. What does the Welshman do? He bellows at his son as if he has committed the greatest sin imaginable. But he puts his arm around his daughter and talks softly to her as if she had done nothing wrong at all. I don't understand it.'

In the Welsh countryside, as in any other countryside the world over, people were always closer to natural rhythms and had a readier and more innocent acceptance of what we are pleased to call the facts of life. Far away from city conventions and fuss, people accepted illegitimacy without anguish, men acknowledged their love-children, and the

children and their mothers suffered no condemnation, no
stigma. All the evidence I have found, in the matter of the
most secret and most talked-about human activity, is that
the Welsh people have always been loving, passionate and
earthy; and they have been lucky enough to have poets to
write it all down in a manner varying from simple to splendid, but always warm and sensual.

'Oh men!' wrote Dafydd ap Gwilym, in the fourteenth
century, of his latest flame, 'was there ever such a loving. Did
Merlin feel desire hotter, Tallesin love a lovelier girl . . .' And
much similar stuff.

An unknown medieval poet, in that golden state of warm
dizziness, wrote:

> Sweet, pure, proper, sugared mouth, I know
> a snug grip for lip-locking.
> My pretty one of the shining brow,
> her lips like clear honey.

Any study of love in Wales reveals ribald and Chaucerian
tales which prove that the Welsh, in this particular matter,
are merely human. They tend to be circumspect in public,
passionate in private. Of course, thin-lipped puritanism
froze some of the rumbustiousness out of the countryside
and chapel strictures introduced a greater element of guilt
into the Welsh way of love; and some of those who, in the
eyes of preachers and deacons were guilty of sexual sin, were
hauled over coals of hypocrisy for public rebuke. On the
other hand, many young men knew perfectly well that certain young women were more amenable to their advances
after an emotional Sunday service in which tensions and
excitement had been heightened; and the sex-appeal of some
ministers and the stimulating effects of their sermons were
well enough known. The good attendances at baptism by
total immersion no doubt stemmed from pious belief, but
may also have had something to do with the way the thin
shifts that young women wore clung so fetchingly to them
when wet. And, of course, hot hymns had sometimes to give
way to the practical and pressing considerations of hot
breath: the custom of bundling, or unsecret courting in bed,

which helped to make long courtships more bearable, was known in the Welsh countryside until the beginning of this century, in spite of the strong grip of the chapels.

While the chapel as an institution has declined, the chapel building, plain as a Sunday suit and sometimes alien and ugly, remains a familiar part of the architectural scene of any Welsh village or town. So, too, does the manse. For more than a hundred and fifty years Welshmen marked their land and their history by sinking mineshafts and raising chapels. The dizzy rise and the protracted fall of coal have been matched only by the ascent and decline of pulpit-power.

Although the influence of the manse has fallen away in recent times, it remains, in subtle ways, a strong thread in Welsh society. The sons of the manse have made their way, in large numbers, into those fields where an ability to communicate, a certain articulateness and manner, are an advantage. They are therefore in teaching and in the mushrooming field of public relations; and, in particular, in the warm and agreeable warrens of BBC Wales and HTV, the commercial television company. Their fathers, from their pulpits, strove to keep the devil in England, to make Wales a no-go area for sin. Their sons today have new pulpits – without the encumbrance of God.

In a sense, in terms of bestowing privilege in the form of educational and social advantage upon those who go through it, the manse in Wales has always been, and still is to an extent, the equivalent of the public school in England. There is no old-school-tie aspect to a manse upbringing, no tribal expectation that people will get jobs, regardless of ability, just because father is a minister. No, it is simply that the manse has always provided, above all, an atmosphere of wide education. Any minister worth his salt has been involved with the complete spectrum of life in his community and was always the centre of it. Thus his children, from an early age, were accustomed to a traffic of people through the front door and grew up hearing discussion on a wide range of subjects: politics and theology, philosophy and local affairs, poetry and human problems. Ministers, on the whole, have been, and are, deeply education-conscious and their children usually grew up with a proper reverence for books and a familiarity with talk of high quality. There was something else, too: the minister had high status in the community. Although in these materialist days the perch of most-esteemed citizen is often occupied by the bank manager, it was previously held by the minister, and, in any case, he remains a chieftain. The result of this is that the sons of the manse have a social position bestowed upon them and are given a mark to live up to. They have always been the chapel princes, expected to do well and pushed to do well, and often they have been the teachers' pets. 'Remember who you are,' their mothers said to these paragons, lovingly adjusting school-tie knots at five to nine. As a stronghold of the Welsh language the manse has conferred another advantage on its sons: good Welsh. Thus the products of the preacher's house, the boys from mission control, are usually self-assured and highly articulate, readily and unselfconsciously bilingual, able to talk with anyone, preordained to be somebodies rather than nobodies: ready-made broadcasting material, telly-people for the post-Christian age.

As things have changed in manse and chapel, so have they changed in the miner's house. Men in their fifties now can remember the time when miners' wives walked a respectful two paces behind their manly bread-winners. Today a lot of miners are to be seen two paces behind their wives, bowed by the supermarket groceries. And young miners borrow their mothers' hairnets to keep their fashionably long hair tucked up inside their helmets and out of harm's way.

Social changes are interesting enough, and Wales has certainly been changing these past ten years, but the quality we call Welshness remains, in a way, unchanging. It is not easy to say exactly what Welshness is because it is both obvious and subtle, clear and elusive, and it is as difficult to describe as to explain the taste of wine to someone who has never drunk it.

We need to bear in mind that Welshness springs from the dynamics of history, culture and religion, the forces of industry and economics. Because these moulding elements have differed in their emphasis and effect in different parts of Wales, we should be clear that Welshness is not something of even consistency spread throughout Wales; and that even to people living in Wales the word Welshness implies different values.

In those areas where the Welsh language is strongest, in north Pembrokeshire, Cardiganshire, Carmarthenshire, Merioneth, Caernarfonshire, Anglesey and parts of Montgomeryshire, Flintshire and Denbighshire, a very large part of Welshness, and some would claim the totality, is rooted in the language itself because the people are using it as the main medium of their expression and thought and daydreaming, and their social and business lives. In these districts it is possible to talk of a Welsh way of life – that is, an existence through the Welsh language, probably a community existence in which social activities play an important part, in which the chapel, the *eisteddfod*, the pursuit of music and poetry are significant facets in the lives of people who base their lives in the countryside. It would be misleading for me to romanticize 'the Welsh way of life' and give an impression that rural Wales is peopled only by sturdy peasants, hill farmers, road menders and coracle stitchers, scribbling epic poems in their lunch breaks and in their lamp-lit evening rest. Nevertheless, there is a powerful element of cultural appreciation, and a tradition, which I think is stronger than in the English countryside. There are certainly many farmer-poets and labourer-poets and cobbler-poets, and the local *eisteddfodau* are well supported and the winners of poetry crowns and prose and music prizes are held in esteem. It all adds up to a rich and important colour in the pattern of Welshness, and the knowledge that it is there seems somehow to make the very landscape alive.

The further east and south you travel in Wales the greater the dilution of language-Welshness. It certainly exists in pockets in some of the valleys and towns, and even Cardiff has its Welsh-speaking enclaves. But, generally speaking, in the industrial valleys of the south there is a Welshness of a different character. It is anchored in the pride that people have in their own communities and in the fact that their background, accent and environment give them a distinctive difference. They have the traditional Welsh sociableness and their choirs and bands. They may not have a lot of Welsh, but their repertoires include many Welsh songs and they are not, in most cases, very far away from the Welsh language. Their fathers and mothers probably spoke it, or their grandfathers; and they may have Welsh-speaking aunts or cousins, and probably they learned some Welsh at school and their children may do the same. This kind of Welshness is harder to measure. It is often expressed in support for the national rugby football team, and this support is an extension of loyalty to the local, the community, team. It is a kind of tribalism. But if you were to ask these Welshmen about their ideas of Wales many of them would talk in terms of the chunk with which they identify mist strongly: east of Llanelli and south of Merthyr Tydfil. They do not identify much with north Wales, an area not well known to most of them, and an area which plays soccer and therefore has a different socio-sporting language. But most acknowledge their Welshness and are proud of it. If you would like to hear the dangerous sounds of teeth being ground, and the creak of skin stretching as fists clench, go into a bar in the Rhondda or the Rhymney, drink someone's pint and suggest that only Welsh-speakers are the true Welsh. Many Monmouthshire men, for example – and Monmouthshire is a county that has spent much of its time cuddling Wales while playing footsie with England – will affirm their Welsh loyalty when the chips are down – usually when the English fifteen and the Welsh fifteen run out on to some hallowed baize while the crowd bays for blood in yet another game of Celts and Saxons, the private thousand years' war. They will be identifying passionately with the rest of the Welsh tribe, but when the singing starts some of them will feel a little uncomfortable, caught up in the fervour, but able only to mouth and clutch at the almost-forgotten or never-learnt words of *Calon Lan* and *Mae Hen Wlad Fy Nhadau*. A lot of Monmouthshire men think the language is a real pain and a total irrelevance. On the other hand, Welsh happens to be the most popular evening class subject in the country.

In the cities and along the coastal belts of north and south Wales, as well as on the middle border, Welshness is further diluted because a large number of the people who live here are not of Welsh origin or are Welsh people who have hacked off their Welshness because they regard it as irrelevant or sentimental or silly. These areas are the most heavily anglicized and are where the Conservative Party has most support in Wales. It is worth noting, when considering Welshness, that a fifth of the people who live in Wales were born outside the country and a seventh of them were born in England. Even in Anglesey, a Welsh language stronghold, a quarter of the population was born in England. In most respects, city Wales and suburban Wales is indistinguishable from city and suburban England: it is substantially English. (Although, to be fair, Swansea has much more of a Welsh atmosphere than cosmopolitan Cardiff.) While there is a certain classlessness in many parts of Wales, which I have always found refreshing, there is naturally an English class system in suburban Wales.

Thus it is not easy to talk of Wales as a uniform unit, any more than it is possible to do so with England. From time to time, foreign newspapers and broadcasting organizations have asked me: 'What do the Welsh think about—?' asking for a brief judgement on a particular matter of moment, as if the Welsh – of all people – would speak with one voice on it. But what Welsh? The Welshman in Cardiff going to see about having his television aerial turned towards an English transmitter? The valley miner, his heart rooted in the old culture, who proudly regards himself as Welsh? The valley miner who thinks Welshness is just sentiment and regards himself only as British? The hill farmer? Or the hill farmer's son off to work in Birmingham?

No, Wales may be a country and a nation, but it is not a tidy parcel. It never has been, nor will be. It is a land of nuances.

Sometimes politicians and writers describe Wales as two countries and by that they mean north and south; or Welsh-speaking and non-Welsh-speaking; or industrial Wales and rural Wales. There is substance in all of these ideas but none of them is completely right. Between the black and white is a vast bolt of greys. A television political commentator mused once: 'If you want to get the feelings of the Tories or the Labour party about a particular issue you take soundings among half a dozen MPs. But if you want to find out something about Wales you have to ask all thirty-six MPs!'

Wales is such a bundle of paradoxes that you dare not be dogmatic about it. There are many people who will have nodded approval to see me write of Wales as a country and a nation. But there are others who would regard that statement as indefensible, who would shout hear-hear to the man who hid behind the pseudonym Union Jack to write to his local paper in the heartland of Wales: 'Sir, When we see headlines like *British Lions Conquer All*, does it not fill you with nostalgia for the time when, as Britain, we could have taken on the world at anything? What with Welsh and Scottish nats trying to fragmentize, is it not obvious that most of us would prefer to remain British? Let us keep our "Welsh" fervour for the singing festival or the pubs and clubs.'

There are others who would agree with the man from Caerphilly who wrote to the London *Observer* '. . . there is no such place as Wales. The area has been part of England since 1536 and most people accept it for the fact it is. The local councillors are as English as anywhere in the rest of England and the population reject the separatist calls of the Nationalists with their silly language . . .'

At this writing the Welsh-speaking population has been declining during the past ten years at the rate of two hundred a week, the damage done by death and depopulation, and, for those who care, it represents a dreadful haemorrhage. Obviously, if depopulation goes on at a great rate and the forces of uniformity, aided by transistor and cathode ray, continue to have great success in Englishing Welsh out of Wales, the kind of Welshness that many Welsh people would regard as fundamental will grow weaker. It is one of the ironies of modern Wales that at a time when the language is more vigorous than it has ever been, and when public regard for it is growing, it is being eroded like a sandcastle before a new tide. And in spite of the unstanched haemorrhage there is the manifest intensification of Welsh consciousness and the growth of confidence.

If we look at some other aspects of Welshness we see that Wales remains a land of welcomes and ready hospitality, a country where the skills and pleasures of talking seem to count for more than in England's pub culture, and where children are encouraged to speak up and say their piece without precocity. Indeed, an undue diffidence in speaking is regarded with some suspicion because it is imagined that you are thinking something nasty when you could be airing it. And Welsh people are curious to know what you are thinking. There is still the tendency, the Celtic tendency, to tell you what you want to hear, especially if you are a stranger, and that, I suppose, is a part of the natural hospitality of Wales. Welsh people say, in reflective moments, that some of their number have a habit of agreeing with you in private before going on to a public platform and disagreeing with you, but, on the whole, the Welsh do not stab you in the back; they would rather battle-axe you from the front.

And let me add, as a counterweight to the rosy picture of a highly cultured and articulate nation, that, as in any part of the United Kingdom, there are plenty of Welsh people whose prime literature is a soccer or rugby match programme, the racing page or a bingo card, that there are children raised in deprived and culturally arid homes, that by no means everyone in Wales looks benignly on cultural pursuits, particularly when there is food to be bought and rates to be paid. There is also the usual suspicion of some of art's loftier reaches, and I am reminded of the Swansea councillor who snorted: 'Ballet? Ballet is just a leg show for the nobs!'

In the same way, let me say that there are limits to the traditional kindness of Welshmen and their great regard for their fellow men. There is an office in Wales where one of the staff is so large and heavy that he is known as Dai Geller for his ability to bend the chairs he sits on. At five o'clock no man in the office wants to be the last to drive off home because that would mean he would be duty-bound to offer the fat man a lift and run the risk of having the passenger seat, or a spring, broken. Thus knocking-off time resembles the start of the Le Mans motor race as the drivers sprint across the tarmac, leap into their machines and ram the accelerators to the floor.

One of the constants of Welsh life, and one of the true parts of the image, is the love of sodality. Community spirit

and a gregarious instinct are in the Welsh genes to a much
greater extent than they are in the English make-up. Outside
Wales, Welshmen quickly join, or form, their Welsh societies and chapels. But there is more to it than that: they
also have a strong attachment to their *bro*, their particular
valley or their street, and when they leave it they feel exiled.
Cardiff has a Carmarthenshire society, but you can drive to
any part of Carmarthenshire from Cardiff in under two and
a half hours. There is even a Rhondda society in Cardiff –
and the Rhondda is only sixteen miles from the capital.
Gwyn Morgan, who works for the European Commission,
recounts with pleasure his encounter with a Welsh hotel
porter in Stratford-on-Avon.

'You're Welsh, aren't you,' the porter said when Gwyn
spoke to him. 'Where do you come from?'

'Aberdare,' Gwyn said, naming his home town with
proper pride.

'Don't generalize, man,' the porter chided, 'what part of
Aberdare – Cwmbach, Robertstown, Trecynon or Aber-
nant?'

Any definition of Welshness ought to include the Welsh
view of the English, and the view, of course, depends upon
where the Welshman is standing. Xenophobia is, in my
judgement, a rare strain in Wales, certainly rarer than in
England. Welshmen, and especially rural Welshmen in the
north-west, feel that they are different from Englishmen and
that in many respects their attitudes and values are better
than English ones. They can identify the differences between
Welshmen and Englishmen – and the composite Englishman turns out to be a bit of a risk-taker, a happy-go-lucky
individual who prefers to spend his money on drink, holidays and generally having a good time. He is class-con-
scious, has an arrogant streak, won't mix readily and keeps
his emotions on a short rein. Even when he is a stranger in a
Welsh district he tends to have a proprietorial air. To a
Welshman a fence is for leaning on for chat; to an Englishman it is to ensure privacy. Most Welshmen are proud of
their Welshness and would not like to be called Englishmen;
but on the whole the English are regarded as good neighbours, if sometimes unfeeling or wilfully ignorant of Welsh

values. It should be said, however, that some people form their opinions after contact with tourists, and holidaymakers are not always the best ambassadors. Although, as I indicated, hostility to the English is on a very small scale, local incidents and certain issues – such as Englishmen buying up cottages in Welsh villages for their holiday homes – can add some fizz to the relationship, and let us remember that some Welshmen have long historical memories and see themselves as the inhabitants of a conquered country. So Englishmen should not take too seriously the famous tribal toast uttered when certain Welshmen forgather to talk and drink: 'Iechyd da pob Cymro, twll din pob Sais.' Which simply means: 'Good health to all Welshmen, arseholes to all Englishmen.' It is rarely said spitefully. There are folk songs which provide a similar outlet like this one:

We like the bonny Scotsman with his tartan and his tam,
We also like the Yankee from the land of Uncle Sam.
But when it comes to Birmingham we couldn't give a
  Dam
And we just don't like the Sais.

And there is another which begins:

Let's be kind to Anglo-Saxons,
To our neighbours let's be nice.
Welshmen, put aside all hatred,
Learn to love the bloody Sais.

Certainly, a lot of Welsh people see in the English a more businesslike and pushing attitude than they themselves possess; although to many highly efficient and commerce-minded Americans and Germans the concept of a pushing and businesslike Englishman is risible. But now, having earlier considered the Welsh and drink, the Welsh and death, the Welsh way of life, and the Welsh and sex, we will consider the Welsh and money. And here, again, we face an array of contradictions.

It seems to many observers that the Welsh have more than their fair share of the congenitally unbusinesslike.

'Do you,' an exasperated Englishman is said to have asked a Welsh shopkeeper, 'have a word in your language that is equivalent to the Spanish term *mañana*?'

'Nothing,' the Welshman replied, 'that conveys quite the same sense of urgency.'

It seems that many Welsh people do not like talking much about the fees that are due to them for services rendered, or the fees that are due to you. Even an Englishman gets round to saying 'How much?' with only a slight reddening of the ears and shuffling of the feet. But many Welshmen seem to take a long time to get round to saying it, and if a Welshman can get a third party to handle the wretched money side then so much the better. He seems to prefer to weave a trail of interconnected debts and credits. The key to the system of unspoken bills is the expectation of a favour in return eventually. There is a story about a group of men in a Welsh pub which illustrates this nicely. The landlord handed a ten-pound note to the doctor in settlement of a long outstanding bill; the doctor gave the note to the butcher to settle a meat bill; the butcher paid the grocer, the grocer paid the garage proprietor for a tyre, the garage proprietor paid the carpenter for shelves, and the carpenter, to clear his slate, gave the note back to the landlord. I heard recently of a north Wales butcher who would only smile reassuringly when an hotelier begged him repeatedly for bills. After two years, the butcher sent in his account: it was, naturally enough, for several hundred pounds. It may be that, in rural Wales especially, the use of currency became established much later than it did elsewhere and that men got into the habit of bartering goods and developing long memories. An uncommercial attitude has a refreshing and appealing aspect in a world so heavily committed to materialism and rake-off; and being congenitally unbusinesslike myself I find myself comfortably in accord with this thread of Welsh life. But *mañana* has its dangers and I have sometimes thought that if the Welsh were ever to become extinct as a nation their epitaph might be They Sent No Bills.

Having said all that, I turn to see the other face of business Wales, and this face has an eye for a profit, a nose for a bargain, an ear for a City rumour. History has many examples of Welshmen with great drive and acumen who have made fortunes at home and abroad, who have propped up on their breakfast table sauce bottles both *Baner ac Amserau Cymru* and the *Financial Times*. It may be that the apparent lack of a commercial edge in Wales, and I lay some emphasis on the word apparent, is that many of those with acumen have left to make their pile. And because Wales has always been a poorer country than England those who stayed behind have had to be rather careful with their limited money. There is good evidence now, however, that the tide is on the turn and that more of the naturally hardheaded are staying in Wales, or returning while still quite young, to start and run businesses and take senior posts in large organizations. This is a healthy sign and it may be that when Wales has an assembly to manage a large sector of Welsh affairs, part of the dynamic of devolution may be the return of many Welshmen to their country. Wales has manufactured plenty of teachers, but it does not have enough home-brewed management and executive material, engineers, chemists, high-technologists, bank managers and industrialists, especially in the Welsh-speaking areas, and companies have had to import men from England to do jobs in these specialized fields.

There is one sector of life in Wales, however, where a ruthless businesslike attitude thrives. In his search for a ticket to an international match at Cardiff Arms Park, a Welshman becomes as commercial as an opium dealer, as heartless as a highwayman, as determined and wheedling and cunning as a cat who has spied cream. This normally generous man, who would prefer to give you something than rent it or sell it to you, who would give you the lamb chop from his plate, would exhume his grandfather if he thought there was a ticket accidentally folded into the shroud. He pulls strings like a crazed campanologist. He calls late at night to remind you of old promises, made in wine. He pursues labyrinthine trails and half-clues like a demented detective. For two or three weeks before a big match the tickets are the kruger rands of Wales. The Post Office and the licensed trade have come to depend heavily on the money spent on telephone calls and heart-softening drinks by the ticketless. Gren Jones, the cartoonist of the *South Wales Echo*, drew a cartoon on the day that Gareth Edwards, the greatest of scrum halves was awarded the MBE, showing a man reading a paper headlined 'Queen Gives Gareth the MBE'. Some people, ran the caption, will do anything to get a ticket! In the nervous days before a big match, security is on a crown jewels scale. Tickets are locked in safes, secreted under pillows, or stitched into underpants. On the day of the match those with tickets are easy to spot: they keep rubbing the back pocket of their trousers to feel the ticket warming within.

The archetypal ticket stories are of two kinds. One is on the theme of the rugby fan getting to Cardiff, finding he has left his ticket at home, rushing back and recovering his ticket from under the mattress, apologizing to his wife who is on it, negotiating her bill with the milkman. The other story is based on the tradition that the man with a ticket always makes it to the match, in spite of fearsome odds. One black tale is about an empty seat in the best part of the stand: an unbelievable occurrence. Two men in the row behind the empty seat grow increasingly agitated at the offensive sight and at last tap the man sitting on the left of it on the shoulder.

'Whose seat is that?'

'It's my wife's.'

'Well, where is she?'

'She's died.'

'Well, dear Moses, man, couldn't you give the ticket to your brother?'

'I did. But he insisted on going to her funeral this afternoon.'

Rugby football plays a considerable part in Welsh life, if you will allow an understatement. For a time, after I arrived in Wales, I tried to avoid contact with the game because I had just left a job which required my attendance in the press boxes at numerous soccer, rugby and cricket matches on behalf of various national newspapers, and I had had a surfeit of sport. I felt that the quality of soccer had declined so much that insanity arising out of boredom would ensue if I saw one more match. Indeed, I have not watched it, in the flesh or on television, since I came to Wales. I rested from rugby for a while, but Welsh rugby is different from any other and eventually I found myself out with all the other bloodhounds sniffing around for a ticket . . .

I do not think that it is mere fancy to say that in some ways Welsh rugby reflects the mood of modern Wales, the new confidence and pride in Welshness. It seems reasonable to relate the so-called golden age in rugby to the new awareness and the shaking off of old shackles. It is curious that a game originated and perfected in English public schools, and first brought to Wales by top-drawer colleges, should become the medium through which generations of Welshmen have poured out so much of their self-expression, emotion and aggression. But it is well suited to the valleys, a game with elements of warfare and poetry and sudden violence, with roles for the heavily muscular and the lightly nimble, a manly game to capture the imagination of men who spent their working lives in cramped holes and danger under the ground, a group game relying on its committees of backs and forwards working together yet leaving spaces for acts of individual heroism or foolishness. It is a game to which Welshmen have contributed their own style: Welsh threequarter and half-back play sprang from the need of stocky men to be elusive and terrier-like when facing men of larger and heavier frame. It was a game which, in its early years, was frowned on by nonconformist puritans who complained about players changing in pubs and said that rugby was 'the fascination of the devil and twin sister of the drinking system'. Such condemnation naturally made the game more popular.

There was something else, too. Rugby was a game that Wales could afford. A relatively poor country like Wales was not able to find the money for a big-business sport staffed by expensive professional players; that is one reason why rugby has always been bigger than association football in south Wales. But, more important, rugby was a game which evolved in the small communities clustered around the pit heads and has been enriched by the deadly rivalries between the villages. A young man pulling on the shirt of his home team is fighting for his dad, his mam, his auntie, his uncle, his granny, his kid brother and Mrs Lewis next door and Mr Jones the Bread. They are all there rooting for him and that is a potent element in Welsh rugby, and something that is missing from professional games where players are bought and sold. Barry John, who became Welsh rugby's first superstar, recalls that he once ignored the loyalty rule and played a match for a team from the neighbouring village and it took him a long time to live it down. When a player pulls on the red shirt of Wales he is still going out to fight for his village folk; add to that the fact that he is also going out to play for his country, and the crowd is laying down an advance barrage of great songs and hymns, then you have powerful forces at work. Moreover, Wales is a small country and small countries need to be noticed. Winning internationals gets you noticed and puts you on a par with coun-

Evan's daughter did well didn't she – married a chap who gets complimentaries!

tries which are able to meet the expense of professional sport. When the opponent is England, it is war. The centuries peel away and the early Middle Ages return and the Welsh warriors run out to bash the Anglo-Saxons and drum them back over the border in disarray. The white card from the Welsh Rugby Union inviting a man to play for his country is the equivalent of the invitation that King Arthur sent to ask a man to join him and the rest of the boys at the round table. Welshmen play rugby for the love of it and some of them are good enough to have the perk of glory as well. When Welsh rugby players meet other sportsmen at dinners, the professional footballers and golfers tell them they are mad to do so much, to train and to entertain the public for nothing. Well, rugby union is an amateur game and, without striving officiously to be completely rigid on that point, Welsh clubs keep it an amateur game. Some players are tempted to play rugby for money in the north of England, and then the rugby union administrators go into an official huff and banish them for ever from Welsh rugby, and at one time even banned them from socializing on Welsh club premises: the administrators of sport sometimes behave like silly old ladies. That apart, Welsh rugby is almost entirely a healthy sport. Its community base makes it very much a game of the people who support it. It contributes to the self-awareness of Welsh people and is a significant focus for their self-expression. Few of its players indulge in the tantrums of soccer's prima donnas – and there is not (yet) such a phenomenon as Welsh rugby hooliganism. Inevitably there is a lot of excitement, some horseplay and some drunkenness among spectators; but crowd behaviour has not degenerated into the kind of mindless violence that scars soccer. Welsh rugby crowds are hotly partisan, and the steam generated at a needle match between two valleys sides has to be experienced to be believed. But feeling has, so far, been vented through the traditional abuse, not fists and bottles. Welsh rugby, like any popular sport, has its superfans who have crossed the line between enthusiasm and obsession, and that is, perhaps the unhealthiest aspect of Welsh rugby; in the end – and you can see I have a taste for heresy – it is only a game.

I was saying: 'It's only a game' to myself as I battled my way to the bar in the Angel Hotel on the day of an international at Cardiff Arms Park. A fifteen-minute breathless push and shove through a mob packed tighter than a scrum, to buy, from a harassed barman, one-sixth of a gill of expensive firewater, which gets reduced through spillage on the way back to the elbow room to one-twelfth of a gill, may strike the incognoscenti, not to mention the teetotal, as a very foolish activity indeed. They are right. It *is* a very foolish activity. But it goes on in most of the hotels and bars in the city centre in the three hours before the match and is as much a part of international day as the kick-off.

Westgate Street, the street outside Cardiff Arms Park, is closed to traffic and filled with a great crowd. The ticket holders, safe and smug, march importantly by. The anguished ticket-less, like minnow shoals, dart this way and that in search of a tout and cry out for tickets like beggars for alms. Once, a tout was upended by desperate men who had travelled far to see the English die the death of a hundred points: they grasped his ankles, hoisted him aloft and shook him so that money and tickets fluttered out like ticker tape. The third main group in the street are the swappers. They have seats in the north stand, but they want to be in the south. They have a south, but they want to be in the north, and they walk up and down shouting their wares.

'North for a south.'
'South for a north.'
'Two enclosures for a stand.'
'What about Gareth's knee?'
'A drop of this'll warm you.'
'Merve the Swerve.'
'That ref – he's learning Braille.'
'Played for Llanelli 1933.'
'My auntie knew Lloyd George.'
'Or was it 1932?'
'She flushed his ticket down the pan.'
'Crikey Moses!'
'No, it was 1931.'
'Grounds for divorce, man.'
'Lovely girl, but—'

'Thick as two blackboard dusters.'

'Dai voted for the council to buy the chandelier.'

'If they could find someone to play it.'

'With that ref they've got sixteen men.'

'Have you met Lord Chalfont?'

Meanwhile, in private rooms in hotels close to the ground, the *crach*,* are finishing their cognac and sambuca at the small lunch parties which are a feature of all international days. Some of the guests are the London Welshmen who have come up for the day to put fresh oil into their Welsh sumps. Like the national *eisteddfod*, the rugby international at Cardiff is an important meeting-place for natives and exiles alike. Although some people may resent the comparison, the social parts of the international and the *eisteddfod* have much in common. And so the crowd streams into that great Welsh wasps' nest to add their voices to the mighty buzz of sound.

In the bars the barmen slump over the pumps, wrung out like chamois leathers, and outside the luckless ticket prospectors admit defeat and flatten their noses against the windows of kindly television rental shops. At one international I stood in the north enclosure, a corral which is the very core of the best singing, as the Irish Christians came out to be eaten by the Welsh lions. It was a cold day, but in that vast press of warm and singing humanity, and close to the breath of young women, I maintained a steady ninety-eight-point-four. Having observed all these Welshmen a little earlier, taking in pints of Brains bitter like Boeings refuelling in mid-air, I marvelled at the elasticity of the native bladder and concluded that there must be significant physiological differences between Welshmen and Englishmen. But at the first shrill vibration of the pea in the referee's whistle at half-time, I was shouldered aside as the anxious mob, like rats to the Weser, streamed to the small dank enclosure which, in the Welsh Rugby Union's main concession to the Welsh language, is also marked *dynion*.†

The path to the Brecon Beacons took me by way of

* The upper-crust, the nobs.

† Gentlemen.

Hirwaun, a village in the foothills, scarred by mining but with fine views for compensation. The people here made a name for themselves after 1973 because they refused to allow the gas authorities to build two large storage tanks close to their homes. Hirwaun broke the rules of the planning game which state that once you have lost your case at a public inquiry you must give in gracefully and watch philosophically, thumbs in braces, as the earth-movers roar in to dig the holes. Hirwaun said to hell with that. The people posted pickets to guard the entrance to the site and stopped the contractors getting on with the job. The pickets worked a rota from dawn until dusk. Mostly, they were housewives, but they were augmented from time to time by off-shift miners and factory workers, and they kept up their picket for more than two years and even mounted guard on Christmas Day in case the gas board tried a daring raid. There is nothing like a struggle with a common aim to unite people, and the picketing became integrated into Hirwaun's way of life and did a lot to stimulate a greater sense of community. The villagers always said that although the regular picket was small, the help of thousands of factory workers and other supporters could be counted on if ever the need arose. And, sure enough, this claim was put to the test. The contractors rolled up with a small task force of vehicles and men, with a police escort, to break through the picket line and establish a bridgehead. At that moment the villagers left their factory benches and their homes and ran in their hundreds to form a warm and flexible human wall. The contractors tried to get through, with the help of the police, but the great wall of Hirwaun withstood the assault. The task force was repulsed and did not return. As I watched the villagers disperse I thought the gas board's only hope was to build an enormous wooden horse and offer to put it on the site as a gesture of friendship. Failing that, and considering the determination of these people, the board would have to look for another site. And in the end that is what it did.

I climbed the steep road to Penderyn and marched on to Ystradfellte which is in the centre of the district of beautiful waterfalls on the Mellte and Hepste rivers. Soon I was looking out over the great panorama of the valley of the Senni and

I scrambled down the slopes into Heol Senni. This valley, too, had been a recent battleground between bureaucrat and local inhabitant and I reflected that Wales was a land of protest as well as song. A farmer gave a shout and asked me to help him round up a straying cow. We cornered the creature in a lane and, as we led it back, the farmer talked of the days when Senni farmers fought a scheme to turn their valley into a reservoir. I remember that at one of these confrontations with authority, a lorry driver from London who was trying to deliver drilling equipment for the water engineers' survey work, was furious. He gazed around at the wide valley. 'Why don't these farmers come to their senses and get out? Why do they want to live in a place like this? There's nothing here. There's nothing to do.' The chasm between city man and rural man is wide. The lorry driver would have been pained to learn that after some months of bloodless guerrilla warfare, the farmers won and the reservoir plan was abandoned. So the Senni valley remains free, to be worked and walked; and I walked through it into Defynog where I stopped in a cool inn for a drink to refresh me for the last lap to Sennybridge, a little town on the edge of the military range which covers most of the wild Mynydd Epynt.

I had walked more than twenty-eight miles that first day and my lower half seemed to have a separate existence, like the equine part of a centaur, and my feet were in a mess. Wynford Vaughan-Thomas had said: Don't forget the socks.

I had forgotten the socks.

When you are walking long distances over rough country you must wear two pairs of socks to prevent blistering; every cub Scout knows that that is elementary. I had worn one pair of socks all day and now I had blisters like soufflés and blood in my boots. Towards the end of the day each step had been a pain and I thought I might end up, pecked clean, under a cairn with a rough shingle ignominiously inscribed 'Died of blisters'. Having learned the hard way, I bathed my cringing, flogged-round-the-fleet feet in surgical spirit and thereafter wore two pairs of socks.

The Army had given me permission to cross Mynydd

Epynt and had told me where I could, and could not, walk. It was a Saturday and so it was unlikely that I would be shelled. There was a small inn on the way, the Shoemakers Arms, and I stopped for a freshener of orange juice. The licensee's wife said that she and her husband had come to this remote nook in Wales to escape from London suburban rat-racing, and they were enjoying themselves immensely.

It was cold on Epynt. The sparse trees are gnarled and hunched like Quasimodos and gang together stubbornly against the weather. The Army has twenty-nine thousand acres up here, a sore point with those who believe the Services own too much of Wales and talk bitterly of dispossession of the farmers. Today, Epynt is not often seen by the public. It is bleak land, yet thrilling in its wildness; remote and empty. The paths are littered with the dross of rehearsed warfare: spent shell cases, ration packets and the dog-ends of thunderflashes. The soldiers have brightened the wilderness by giving the narrow and broken tracks homely and incongruous names. I walked up Gun Park Road, past Burma Road to Dixie's Corner, then up Piccadilly to Piccadilly Corner. There was no Eros here, just a bad-tempered old ram bleating his annoyance; and no people either. This is the lonely land once criss-crossed by the droving ways, the trails of the cattle drovers who were important men in the commercial life of Wales for six hundred years. Up here now, it was easy for me to imagine the herds of black cattle, two or three thousand head at a time, being urged across this Welsh veldt on their way to the Midlands, to London and the south-east of England, bellowing and grumbling, with the Welsh cowboys shouting *'Heiptrw Ho!'* The cattle, shod with iron, clattered over the stony roads. The drovers avoided the turnpike toll roads when they could because of the high cost of getting their animals through; and all the way from Wales through England their routes are still marked by inns called Drovers Arms and Drovers Rests and by roads called Welsh Way. On the whole the drovers were men of substance, tough and shrewd certainly, but not irresponsible roughnecks. They were licensed to drive cattle and had to be worthy to get a licence. They carried goods and mail in both directions, and news,

too. They founded banks to handle their business, like the
Aberystwyth and Tregaron Bank, known as the Black Sheep
Bank because its two-pound notes bore a picture of two
black sheep and the ten bob note bore a portrait of a lamb.
The railways put an end to the overland droving, to the
colourful story of the trail bosses and the Welsh wild west;
and no doubt the respectable householders of some English
towns and villages were relieved that the regular invasions
by the Celts and their cattle had come to an end.

When I came down from Epynt's moors I walked through
the Crynach forest and scrambled down a hill, waded
through a stream, and came at last to the Dol-y-coed hotel in
the faded old spa of Llanwrtyd Wells where the clock seems
to have stopped some time before the First World War. The
town became a fashionable watering-place after a local vicar
noted the extraordinary gymnastics of frogs who had drunk
from the sulphur springs. But the pump rooms that were
once a facility in the hotels are no longer working. With
twenty miles notched that day I felt rather like the tired
drovers who used to rest up at Llanwrtyd and I took five
cups of tea like a horse at a municipal trough, and quite
shortly afterwards a large bowl of leek soup, a slab of new
salmon, some fruit pie and a generous spoonful of Stilton,
and then a glass of Dublin whiskey, before falling, like a
felled pine, into bed in a quaint black-beamed room that
had sheltered travellers for four hundred years.

In the morning, as arranged, Colin Jones, a local butcher,
was waiting outside with two ponies, Ringo and Passion
Flower. Ringo agreed to carry me and we set off in heavy
rain to the Abergwesyn Pass and along the narrow and
lovely road through the valley of the Irfon, a trout and
salmon stream. This is prize-winning country by any standard and the Nature Conservancy holds a good stretch of it,
so that the land stays rugged and red and yellow and rocky
where the conservancy writ runs. But the Forestry Commission has planted a lot of conifers in the district and you
can see these trees peeping up on the skyline, like Apaches in
a Western. The rain beat down more heavily on us, shaping
our hats into cloches. We passed a drenched shepherd who

waved his crook in rueful greeting, and we skidded and clattered up the Devil's Staircase, a steep and twisting kink in
the road.

'Pony trekking,' Colin Jones said, the water running from
his nose and chin, 'is a great way of spending a holiday and
it makes a great difference to life in Llanwrtyd. The hotels
and guest houses depend a lot on it, and I make a living
selling them joints and chops and steaks. It is the right kind
of tourism for our district, not too big, not too noisy, not
brash. It fits in with country life and provides work for the
local people. It helps to keep the district alive and the community together.'

Llanwrtyd may have struck a balance – but, farther south,
in the Black Mountains area of the Brecon Beacons, the
phenomenal growth of pony trekking has caused problems.
So many riders go out that paths are worn out and farmers
and graziers and walkers grow angry about the damage and
the pony-jams. Anxious to bring peace to the area, the
Countryside Commission and the national park committee
decided to spend twenty-five thousand pounds on an inves-
tigation into the problem and the working out of a solution
to it.

Half-way between Llanwrtyd and Tregaron Colin Jones
had to turn back, as we had arranged, and I walked on along
the winding road. Rain squalls hissed and the wind howled
and my boots slopped through the rivulets running across
the road. The water here feeds into the infant river Tywi
which, in turn, feeds the Llyn Brianne reservoir a few miles
down the valley. The reservoir and its dam are one of the
largest water projects in Britain and the road to it has
opened to a large public some of the most splendid landscape in Britain. The Brianne reservoir represents a victory
for the people who, during the nineteen-fifties, fought one of
the classic Welsh water battles. The plan at that time was to
flood part of the Gwendraeth valley in the southern part of
Carmarthenshire, but the local people objected to the loss of
land and homes – and when the water surveyors approached
the church bells were rung in warning and the people bolted
gates and blocked entrances. In the end the water authorities
had go elsewhere and they found Brianne where the drown-

ing of the *cwm* did not involve dispossessing anyone of his home or taking a lot of productive farmland. Moreover the water is for the benefit of Wales and there was no question, as there was elsewhere in Wales, of an English industrial town helping itself to a valley.

The Llyn Brianne scheme also provides something unique in wildlife conservation, a regular bus service for commuting salmon. Because the three-hundred-foot high Brianne dam is an obstacle that even Welsh salmon cannot surmount, and the spawning grounds are three or four miles upstream, the salmon and sewin – sea trout – which come racing up the Tywi on urgent business, now collect in a trap, or waiting-room, a few hundred yards below the dam. Every day the trap is emptied and the fish are transferred to an aerated tank on an adapted Land Rover and are then driven up to their spawning grounds. Later, a return service operates to take the fish back downstream. Without this scheme the fish population would be seriously depleted and the Tywi's reputation as one of the great salmon rivers of Europe would be lost. The salmon and sewin make the Tywi a rich river in material terms, too – riverside land with fishing rights changes hands for what seems to many local people to be fabulous sums.

Down river, around Carmarthen town, the coracle men still go about their business as they have done in Wales for perhaps twenty centuries. A hundred years ago there were thousands of coracles working Welsh rivers, but fishing laws, the angling lobby and the interests of conservation, have reduced the number drastically and coracles have vanished from the Usk, Wye, Severn, Dee, Cleddau, Conwy, Dyfi, Nevern and Loughor and other streams. Today there are nineteen licensed coracle nets – two coracles per net – working on the Teifi, the Taf and the Tywi, and most are on the Tywi. Although the coracle has been in decline, it seems unlikely that it will become extinct, at least in this century. Certainly, fewer fishermen's sons have been inclined to devote years of watching and listening to absorb ancestral skills and secrets but there is always a considerable demand for the coveted licences when they become available. Raymond Rees, a civil servant and a coracle fisherman for more than twenty years, has a workshop in Ffordd y Cwrwg (Coracle Way) in Carmarthen, and builds his craft in the traditional way, having learned the art from his grandfather who was honoured with the MBE for services to coracle fishing. His materials cost about ten pounds and he may take ten days to make a new boat. The language of coracle fishing is Welsh and all the parts of the craft have Welsh names. (For their amusement, and for pin money, coracle men sometimes make model coracles and sell them or give them as presents. They have been astounded to see, in local shops, the first plastic coracle models – from Japan.)

To build a coracle Mr Rees selects and cuts an ash tree and has it sawn into thin and springy planks. It takes sixteen of these to make the ribs. Willow or hazel sticks are plaited for the gunwale and the frame is skinned with calico and then coated with pitch. Long ago, the coracles were covered with hide, and a fifteenth-century poem talks of a 'paunchy vessel . . . made of a bullock's tunic'. Mr Rees makes his nets, spins cowtail hair for net rope and cuts cow horn for net rings. He has a lead mould for making net weights that belonged to his great-great-grandfather. With a leather carrying strap, a paddle and a small club – the *cnocer* – to stun the fish, the fragile and vulnerable little basket-boat, light as a leaf on the water, and easy enough for a man to carry on his back, is ready.

The coracles sit on the water, about thirty feet apart, with the trawl net between them, and drift downriver for about a mile. They repeat this process two or three times during each expedition, humping the coracles on their backs to reach the starting position. The secret of successful fishing lies in the correct weighting of the net according to the conditions and it is most effective when gliding over the river bottom. A list of legal and natural conditions have to be met before the coracle men can put their craft on their backs and head for their particular stretch of the river. Tywi men, for example, fish from St David's Day, the first of March, until the last day of August, but they may not fish at weekends. Because the fish would see the net by day, the men go out at night, or in daylight if the river is muddy after rain. They may make two or three trips a week. The time when the conditions of law, tide, wind, depth and darkness combine favourably, to make fishing possible, is known as *clyfwchwr*. 'With luck you might catch two fish in a night,' Mr Rees said. 'The largest salmon I ever caught was thirty-two pounds and about four feet long. On the other hand I have been out twenty times in a row and caught nothing. Fishing is a spare-time occupation for coracle men. Usually they sell their salmon and sewin locally, but profits tend to be small. Nobody is in it purely for the money because there simply isn't that much to be made. For me, the fascination of the coracle is in using the ancient skills and the ancient terms, not only in fishing, but in building the craft.'

Coracles may be frail-looking, but they are really very tough and water-worthy. Recently, two Teifi river coracles were paddled by intrepid men, the Welsh navy, across the English Channel, to the amazement of the English and French. The expedition was partly to publicize a protest over the phasing out of coracle fishing in the Cardiganshire village of Cenarth on the order of the river authority which wanted to concentrate the coracles further down the Teifi.

Coracle fishing, as you might expect, is not only rich in lore, but in superstitions also. Fishermen know full well that if they see a minister of religion walking on the river bank, their nets will remain empty. They also tell visitors that worn-out coracles have to be burned beside the river, as an offering to the river gods – and who are they to take chances with the ancient and ordained rhythms and customs of the river? – and anyone who thinks they burn them just to get rid of them has no romance in his soul.

Along the road to Tregaron, I crossed into Cardiganshire, the piggy-bank of Wales. I have written earlier about the lack of a commercial attitude in rural Wales, but I have to confess that Cardiganshire – if reputation and legend are evidence enough – contradicts some of what I said. In this county, it is claimed there are only two institutions for which a man has true reverence. Thus, he removes his hat respectfully on entering the chapel – and the bank; the true Cardi bows only to God and sovereign. In all the stories and jokes, the Cardis emerge as the Scots of Wales (which is an odd way of putting it, I suppose, but that is how it was put to me); and the tales they tell against themselves, of their supposed stinginess and wickedly shrewd business deals, are a traditional part of Cardiganshire humour.

'You can be sure I've looked very carefully at the financial aspects of this,' said John Morris, the Secretary of State for Wales, outlining a new policy. 'After all, I'm a Cardi.'

A company director said to me: 'There's no wild spending in my firm ... we've put a Cardi in charge of the accounting.'

If, in Wales, someone calls you an old Cardi, he means that your slowness to pay for a round of drinks has been noted. The Cardis, it is said, have long pockets and short arms; and when a Cardi is found, apparently dead, a silver coin should be placed in his palm: if the fingers do not clench to grasp the coin within a minute or two then life may be pronounced extinct with absolute safety. Cardis themselves like to say they install wall-safes rather than television sets and that Scrooge and Shylock visit Cardiganshire regularly for refresher courses. There is a tale of two confidence tricksters who were arraigned in court charged with perpetrating frauds in twelve of the thirteen counties of Wales; the thirteenth charge, relating to Cardiganshire, concerned only an *attempted* fraud.

While Cardiganshire has been generous in giving the world a host of sea captains, milkmen, teachers, preachers, and poets, the people have earned a reputation for dedicated eking. If we look at their history and the shape of the land we can see why. For many centuries the people earned a bare living off the hard hills and it became a tradition for young people to leave as soon as they were able, to earn their living elsewhere. The tradition is still strong today: the county has the highest proportion in England and Wales of schoolchildren who go on to higher education. Many of those who emigrated had their first taste of the outside world. when they joined the drovers on the great cattle drives to England. The Cardis who made regular runs with the cattle brought back the money to buy land – and they also brought back the latest fashions from London, so that some Cardi girls were trend-setters in Wales. From cattle driving there developed the tradition of the Cardiganshire milkman in London, which lasted until the nineteen-forties. Indeed, so many men went from Cardiganshire to start milk rounds in London that one enterprising fellow was able to set himself up in business as a milk-round broker, buying and selling rounds for his fellow Cardis – the milk-Mafia. And alongside this tradition grew the sour stories of watered milk. It was said cynically that Cardi fathers told their London-bound sons: 'Boys, make money. Make it honestly if you can. But, boys, make money.'

For some Cardis, of course, London became home, but they retained their nostalgic longing, the *hiraeth*, for Wales, and could not bear the thought of being buried in London. They always hoped to make their pile and return home in great triumph to live out their days in the valleys of their boyhood. But some left it too late – and when the coin-in-the-palm test had been carried out they made their last journey to Wales, horizontal.

Of all the people of Wales the Cardis have perhaps the strongest sense of root and of county. They are clannish, have a distinctive accent, and for their wanderings and their acumen they have been called the Ibos, or the Jews, of Wales. During the coal epoch of the nineteenth and twentieth centuries thousands of them migrated to the mining valleys of Glamorgan, Monmouthshire and Carmarthenshire. They tended to stick together for many years and stayed close to the chapels. With the Sunday-school virtues of hard work and self-improvement tattooed into their souls, and their knowledge of the poverty back home in Cardiganshire, they saved carefully. They knew the value of a penny because they knew hard times and some of them used to complain that people in South Wales did not know how to handle money properly. They were scandalized by the sight of valleys Welshmen piling coal on to their fires, and Cardis today can recall their parents chiding them: 'Go easy on the coal – you're not in south Wales now, you know.'

Englishmen used to go to Cardiganshire under the impression that they would find there only simple and trusting peasants. But they were often educated with a jolt. An

Englishman once said to a Cardi that he would like to buy some of his farmland.

'How much?' the Cardi asked.

The Englishman looked around at the rolling hillside.

'About a hundred pounds' worth,' he suggested.

'Come back tomorrow, then,' the Cardi said evenly. 'And bring a wheelbarrow.'

Cardiganshire's weather was particularly hostile this day and I was glad to reach Tregaron and to put up at the Talbot Hotel, one of the inns where George Borrow really did stay during his famous tour of Wales in 1854 in which he was a sort of forerunner of Ronay. A sample breakfast enjoyed by

Borrow: 'There was tea and coffee, a goodly white loaf and butter; there were a couple of eggs and two mutton chops. There was broiled and pickled salmon – there was fried trout – there were also potted trout and potted shrimps. Mercy upon me!' Mercy upon his stomach.

Tregaron is an amiable and well-worn country town with an important pony trekking business centred upon it, and I went to see Dr Arwyn Williams who, until his death a few weeks later, was chairman of the local trekking association. He had been one of the last of the horseback doctors in Britain. Until the late nineteen-forties many of the roads to the more remote hill farms in the district were too poor for cars and Dr Williams rode to visit his patients, setting bones and stitching gashes on scrubbed kitchen tables, and looking after injured animals, too, because a country doctor also had to be something of a vet. 'Pony trekking is an important part of our economy because many of the farmers, the farmers' wives, the shopkeepers and the guest-house keepers have a stake in it. A trekking holiday is not expensive and it is an industry on a scale to fit the countryside. It doesn't intrude and it involves people and helps to keep our small communities alive. Our trekking association has rules that ensure that high standards are maintained and that is one reason why trekking is so popular. Trekking holidays bring ten thousand pounds in fees into this area, and I suppose that the trekkers spend about ten thousand pounds in the shops and inns. In a country area it all adds up to a tidy sum.'

I called in at an inn, to further my knowledge of the texture of the neighbourhood. Two men related to me the story of a gander, a quite ferocious creature which had recently attacked a local tradesman.

'Vicious brute, mind. Bit him—'

'Right through his trousers.'

'On his john thomas.'

'He came here first, told the landlord what happened.'

'The landlord laughed.'

'Said it was the early bird—'

'That catches the worm.'

'Poor chap didn't think that was funny.'

'So the landlord gave him a brandy for the shock.'
'He went to the doctor.'
'What with the pain and swelling.'
'Doctor said he'd seen nothing like it—'
'In forty years.'
'The poor fellow's wife said she didn't mind—'
'If the doctor took away the pain.'
'As long as he left the swelling.'

Next day, Rhys Jones, a sheep farmer and mountain guide, awaited me in the town square beside the statue of Henry Richard, the Merthyr MP born in Tregaron. Rhys had two ponies with him, Blackie and Dick, and said that Blackie's grandfather had won the Derby and I saw no reason why I should disbelieve him. We rode out into the hills in fine sunshine and after a while, warm and thirsty, we stopped at an isolated cottage and a woman brought us a glass of water each. 'You'll come to no harm drinking water,' Rhys promised. 'As long as it's Welsh.' He spends part of his summers taking trekking parties out and enjoys the work – and visitors enjoy his sense of humour and evident love of the land. He is one of six brothers, four of whom work on the land that has been in the family for centuries. Hill farming can be tough, but Rhys likes the independence it gives him and would not like the strict timetables of the cattle farmer. The brothers own three sheepdogs each and Rhys said a man needed at least three, maybe four, to work sheep properly. 'I spend a lot of my time training dogs. They are ready to work by the age of two, and then they work for five years or so before they become worn out and have to be put down. A good working dog might fetch a hundred pounds and I know a shepherd who recently refused five hundred pounds for a really good one.'

We rode down to Strata Florida, or, in Welsh, Ystrad Fflur, the flowery way, where Cistercian monks built their abbey in the twelfth and thirteenth centuries and where there was once a great trade in sheep, cattle and lead from the nearby hills. We walked for a while among the abbey ruins and looked at the grave of Dafydd ap Gwilym, one of the greatest of the medieval poets of Europe, who divided his time, sensibly, between making verse and love. He was a poet of the summertime and wrote often of taking young women to stately couches beneath canopies of green leaves; and wrote of his own burial 'in the shade of the soft leaves and the fresh trees, in a shroud of summer clover'. George Borrow had felt moved enough to kiss the yew which shades ap Gwilym's grave, but, being less demonstrative, I thought that a reassuring pat was enough. I also went to see the grave, nearby, of Sir David James, the Cardi millionaire and philanthropist who, some years before his death in 1967, paid for the mighty black monument which is his modest last resting-place. Carved upon the shining black stone in golden letters is the legend: 'Sir David John James. A God-fearing man, philanthropist and patron of Welsh culture.' In the village of Pontrhyfendigaid, just down the road, there is a memorial to the great benefactor's wife, who predeceased her husband. It is in the form of a large stained-glass window in the community centre and depicts the lady in her pearl necklace and fur coat.

Apropos of nothing but graves, there is also buried at Strata Florida a man's leg. The other three-quarters of him lived on in America, the leg left behind inspired a poem by John Ormond.

We mounted up again and rode to the high slopes above the Teifi pools and, in mid-afternoon, found Mr William Owens' farm at Tynddol. Mr Owens welcomed us with tea, cheese and fruit cake, and then offered to put me on the hill track to Ponterwyd, my next overnight stop. He saddled his pony and, with dogs scampering beside us, the three of us rode over the mountain. After a mile or two we stopped because it was time for Rhys to return with Blackie. I dismounted and Mr Owens showed me how to find Coed Bwlchgwallter and the River Ystwyth. The two men turned and were soon small silhouettes on the skyline. I moved quickly down the slopes of wild moor, crossed Nant Ffin and made my way around the edge of the forest. I gambled, turned into the forest hoping for a short cut, but the path I found petered out in a plantation, and there seemed to be disagreement between the map and reality. Admitting that I was lost, I put my trust in the compass and plunged into the trees in an effort to find the river. I did – but first I had to scramble down a cliff of scree, a descent of more than a hundred feet which I accomplished mainly on hands and backside. I crossed the river at Dologau and went up past the chapel near Hafod where once a sculptor made a statue of a mother and child, as a memorial, but put the mother's wedding ring on the wrong finger and, poor perfectionist soul, killed himself.

Now I marched to Devil's Bridge, and being a waterfall-phile clicked through the old turnstile to see the great falls of the Teifi and the Mynach, one of the sights of Wales. Exhilarated, I emerged from the gorge, set stuns'ls and made a fast journey over the four miles to Ponterwyd, to the George Borrow Hotel and to a dinner of steak and blackcurrant jelly. Later I had a talk with the last High Sheriff of Cardiganshire – the last because the county was soon to be swallowed up in the new super-county of Dyfed – and he said he was worried about the spread of the conifer forests. There was a chorus of assent, and, wherever I travelled in mid-Wales, men expressed their concern about the way the forests were altering the texture of the landscape and taking sheep country out of use. I have no doubt that that night I slept in Borrow's room, and I am sure that everyone else in the hotel had that same certainty.

Next day's walk was glorious. Having kept gentlemen's hours at the hotel, I had to walk fast to the Nant-y-moch. reservoir. In a cottage near here was born Sir John Rhys, who got his early schooling in classes at local farms and rose to be professor of Celtic at Oxford university from 1877 to 1915; as a marvel of industrious youth he was for years held as an example to Welsh schoolchildren. He is also remembered for the douche-like comment he made on hearing that Oxford students had been asking for better bathing facilities. 'Baths?' he cried. 'Baths? Good heavens – you're only here for eight weeks at a time!'

I skirted the northern side of Plynlimon and made my way up the valley of the Hengwm river. This was wilderness, wild and haunting, with rushing streams and old farms with caved-in roofs. On the way to Lake Bugeilyn I met a shepherd and checked my bearings with him. I walked around the remote still pools of Bugeilyn and Glaslyn, descended to Aberhosan and walked beside the Dulas to Machynlleth. I stopped for a chat with a man doing some ditching and he asked if I spoke Welsh. I said not much, and he said: 'I'd rather talk in Welsh, but I'm afraid that people like me are in the minority. We should do more about teaching Welsh in the schools. People of my generation did not do enough. We didn't have enough pride. We should have more pride in what belongs to us. We don't want to force other people to learn our language, but we do want to keep what is ours.'

From Machynlleth, next morning, I walked to Pennal and then over the hill track to Tywyn. It had been my aim for some time to ride the Cambrian coast railway – I had written so much about the battle by local people to prevent its closure that I thought I really ought to try it out – and so I bought myself a ticket to Fairbourne, three stations up the line. The Cambrian must count as one of the finest train rides in Europe. The track is poised between the mountains and the sea, and in the diesel cars you have the sensation of flying as you swoop over the beaches and look down on egg-warming seagulls who look up at you with schoolmarm's glares. From Fairbourne's tiny station I walked over the bridge that crosses the estuary of the Mawddach river. The view from here is magnificent, the sands, sea and mountains in harmony, and geese Peter Scott-ing across the sky. For spectacle it must rate as the best threepenny walk in Wales.

I headed for the Rhinog mountains by way of Llanbedr. Near here is Salem chapel, the setting of perhaps the most popular Welsh scene ever painted. It depicts Welsh women at prayer and was painted by Curnow Vosper for the Sunlight Soap Company in 1908. It has now become a part of folk-lore because, it is said, you may spy the face of the devil himself in the shawl of one of the women . . . and that is the so-called 'terror of the Salem picture'. I was soon among the rocks of the Rhinogs, mountains that were made, they say, by God in a temper. Experienced hill walkers reckon that these crags, populated by wild goats, are the toughest country south of the Isle of Skye. I kept to the easier paths and reached the hillside which affords a splendid view of the

Glaslyn estuary and of Portmeirion, the figment of imagination that has been translated into reality by the extraordinary architect Sir Clough Williams-Ellis. I had recently
lunched with Sir Clough, who was then ninety, and his wife,
Amabel, at their home, Plas Brondanw, and Lady Williams-
Ellis recounted the adventures she had had during her recent
journey to Katmandu where she had attended a course in
meditation. She admitted that, at the age of eighty, she had a
little difficulty in adopting the cross-legged lotus position.
We supped stinging-nettle soup, which I had not tasted
before, and I reminded Lady Williams-Ellis that the last
time she had invited me to lunch she had said there would be
wart-hog and hartebeeste on the menu. Unfortunately she
could not get any wart-hog, or indeed hartebeeste, so she
made do by feeding me on soya compounds, fungus, clover
leaf protein, some fishmeal and various morsels grown on
oil waste and pulped newsprint. That particular luncheon
had been the outcome of several months of experiment by
Lady Williams-Ellis and some friends, and it was a contribution to the work being done in many parts of the world
to tackle the problems of malnutrition. The theory was that
people living in areas of chronic food shortage would be
helped by having their diets filled out with protein developed from soya beans, oil waste and other sorts of sludge.
But the key to the whole thing is food-acceptability and the
aim was to demonstrate to people in famine-prone parts of
the third world that westerners would eat this new-fangled
stuff with relish, that it had prestige and wasn't simply
second-rate substitute food to be pushed down the throats of
the suffering. (The idea of cooking wart-hog and hartebeeste
was to interest western people in the possibilities of game
ranching.) Having listened to Lady Williams-Ellis's theory,
and grasped the point, I was ready to bite the bullet. Thus I
found myself at an 'unorthodox food lunch' at Portmeirion,
where the staff are much more used to doing inspired things
to lobsters, trout and steak. The hors d'oeuvre was something grown on oil waste and newsprint: it was possible I
was going to eat my own words. The waiter looked down his
nose at my dunderfunk of curried extruded protein and
fungus, my *plat du jour* of the twenty-first century, and said

with the studied dignity that only waiters can muster:
'Red wine, white wine, or Alka Seltzer?'

I remember that I stayed that night in one of Portmeirion's little cottages and was awoken at daybreak by the
sunlight streaming through the window. I gazed out at the
estuary; the tide had receded and the sands were gleaming.
Out there, on the sands, was a woman, walking slowly, bare-
foot, head up, seemingly entranced, a mature woman in a
diaphanous white négligée, her hair flowing and majestic
breasts jutting; it was like a vision of Isadora Duncan. I put
it down to either a piece of Portmeirion's routine magic, or a
surfeit of clover leaf compound and curried extruded protein.

For a while I shopped at Minffordd to admire one of the
steam locomotives and train of little red carriages of the
Ffestiniog narrow-gauge railway, which is one of the seven
famous small railways of Wales. The trains, all steam and
gleam, puff busily among the hills and waterfalls, making
an increasingly important contribution to the holiday industry. They are not toy railways. They were built as working
commercial lines, and they are full of small and piquant
facts and unique features. The Ffestiniog railway, which
runs from Porthmadog to Dduallt, still uses what is thought
to be the oldest working steam locomotive in the world,
built in 1863. The Snowdon mountain railway which runs
for almost four and three-quarter miles from Llanberis to the
mountain-top still used four locomotives with which it
started in 1896, and is the only rack railway in Britain. The
Vale of Rheidol railway, which snakes from Aberystwyth to
Devil's Bridge, was built in 1902 to carry ore from Cardiganshire's lead mines to the coast. It still uses one of the
original locomotives and is the only narrow-gauge line oper-
ated by British Rail and the only British Rail steam line.
The Talyllyn railway, which runs from Tywyn to Aber-
gynolwyn, is another former slate railway and two of its
original locomotives, built in 1866, and four coaches of that
period, are still running. The Welshpool and Llanfair Caerei-
nion railway was a farmers' line which opened in 1903 and
closed in 1956, but was rescued by a preservation society

and reopened in 1963. There is a splendid ride to be had on the line which runs from Llanuwchllyn along the shore of Bala Lake, and on the smallest of the little railways, the Fairbourne, which has a track gauge of fifteen inches. This line was built to carry building materials in the last century and runs almost a mile and three-quarters in the estuary of the Mawddach.

The rescuing of small steam railways has the appearance of being a very English activity because so many of the volunteers who have come to Wales to revive and operate these picturesque lines are an assortment of bank managers, clerks, lawyers – executives from suburban England who, when they pause to indulge in a daydream at their ledgers, dream of puffs of steam among distant Welsh hills. They give up weekends and holidays to be a signalman, or drivers or guards or gangers, or spit-and-polishers; who would guess that for a considerable number of pinstriped professional men at work in the soft underbelly of England, happiness is an oily rag, a smut on the cheek, and Wales. But the appeal of the steam railways is rather more than a mere extension of small-boy imagination. There is more to it than mountain air, the aesthetic pleasure of watching or working with a steam engine, and pure nostalgia. There is also the fact that those who volunteer to work on the little railways become a part of a community. They regard themselves, not as railway enthusiasts, because that term seems to mean spectators who do little but admire; they think of themselves as railwaymen, even if part time, running a proper railway. Anyone who talks sniffily about boys and their toy trains could find himself lashed down across the narrow gauge on some lonely stretch. Of course, all the railways have to keep to high standards of maintenance and safety, and the romance of steam and takings at the ticket office have to be balanced against rising costs, a fairly short peak season, and heavy bills for maintaining elderly locomotives. Not to mention all the perspiration and the risking of hernias and slipped discs that has gone into getting the disused lines into good order. Many of those city-based railway supporters may be seen from time to time working like navvies with shovels, picks and hammers. The work going on at the present time on the Ffestiniog railway must rank as one of the great amateur civil engineering feats of all time. Part of the old track lies under a lake created for a power station and work is going on to restore the line to Blaenau Ffestiniog by building a new stretch. The teams doing this work started in 1965 and they hope to hack and shovel their way through to Blaenau, like old-time navigators, by 1978.

In Blaenau's nineteenth-century heyday, the years of the great slate rush, slates from the quarries were carried on the railway to Porthmadog harbour, and from here were shipped out to roof the world. Welsh slates were not the cheapest but they were the best in the world and were available in red, grey, blue, green and purple. In 1898 there were sixteen thousand men working in the quarries of north Wales, nine thousand of them in the Blaenau district, and the output from the region was more than two million tons a year. In the lightless 50° Fahrenheit caverns deep in the cores of mountains the men toiled to get the slate out in great baulks; these were sawn into smaller pieces suitable for man-handling and then sent to the slate maker for splitting and dressing. You can still see, in what is left of this once great industry, the craftsmanship of the slate maker: with smart chisel blows he cracks off the thin plates, six or eight to an inch, as if peeling the cards from a stiff new pack. The largest slates are called princesses, the medium ones are marchionesses and countesses, and the smallest ones are ladies.

Around the winning of slate, as with the mining of coal in south Wales, there developed a special breed of men, a way of life, an exclusive vocabulary – the language of slate-working is Welsh – a tradition and an industrial epoch. Many of the young men lived in hillside barracks and, at lunch times, most of the men gathered in their huts, or cabans, which developed into small busy hives of education, and appreciation of literature. In these cabans the men recited and polished their poetry, read to others and debated religion and politics, and elected their chairmen, secretaries and treasurers. They scraped together pennies to help pay for the university college at Bangor, and their ideas and ideals played an important part in the development of radical liberal political thought. Today, the mighty and gleaming heaps of slate waste around towns like Blaenau and Bethesda are monuments to an era. Somehow, unlike the sullen tips of coal waste in southern Wales, these heaps have a dramatic aspect that outweighs ugliness. The slate industry itself has shrunk. In Blaenau, fewer than two hundred men work in the quarries, but there is a small and fairly steady demand for slate for floors, sills, fireplaces, ornaments, and, of course, roofs. But slate roofing costs more than hand-made tiling and, in a way, it has become a luxury material rather like marble. And yet, for all the evidence of decline and the towering piles of slate waste and the gouged-out cliffs, Blaenau and other slate districts have become tourist attractions. The Llechwedd mine at Blaenau, still a working mine, now runs tram tours of the workings and you climb aboard the clanking tram and vanish into a hole in the mountainside, rather like riding a ghost train. On the rock are the carved initials and the marks of the hand-worked drills of the men who worked here more than a century ago. You can see a cavern which is a hundred and fifty feet from floor to roof. There are other caverns much larger, but inaccessible now because of tunnel flooding, and in one of the largest, in the heart of the mountain, there was once a firework display, the rockets sizzling and exploding against the black roof, darker than any sky.

I felt I could hardly pass through Beddgelert without seeing Gelert's grave. Gelert, after all, is better known in Wales than Lassie, Black Bob or Rin-Tin-Tin, and if all the tea towels which carry his picture and his legend were knotted together they would stretch from Beddgelert to Cruft's. Gelert should be the patron dog-saint of baby-sitters, and his story is a solemn warning against drawing hasty conclusions from circumstantial evidence. Gelert was left in charge of a prince's son and when a wolf crept in the door, in order to eat the child, Gelert, the forerunner of all Securicor beasts, naturally killed the intruder. Home came the prince, saw the empty cradle (the child having been tipped out in the struggle), and the blood around Gelert's jaws. Gelert, poor mutt, sat there with a winning look and a wagging tail, expecting a pat on the head and a bone. Today, of course, he would have won the Dickin Medal, the canine VC, but all he received was a death-blow from the sword of the prince, who had deduced that Gelert had feasted on his heir. In the last reel, the prince heard his baby's cry, found the bad wolf's body, put two and two together, and was filled with remorse. Gelert had a decent funeral and the town was named after him; though, no doubt, he would sooner have had a bone.

While I was on the way to Caernarfon, through the big country, a car pulled up beside me and the driver asked if I would mind having a religious pamphlet. I took one. 'Beautiful country, Wales,' he remarked. With many problems, I answered. 'Jesus solves all problems,' he said.

Whether happy in the sunshine, or grumpy in the rain, tranquil or wild, the mountains of this region never fail to move me, to enhance imagination and spirits by at least ten per cent. Photogenic and evocative, relatively unspoiled by electricity pylons and Coke signs, they are a natural hunting-ground for film-makers. They have been passed off as the mountains of Scandinavia, Scotland, America, Europe and China; and they have echoed often to the smack of clapperboard and the shouts of actors dressed as Vikings, paratroopers, guerrillas, barons and witches. For local people, who provide food, drink and other services, the film-makers are a welcome and colourful, if irregular, source of income. Some people have earned fees as extras. Perhaps the most famous extra was the late Mr Wil Napoleon who appeared in several films. He made life a little difficult for staff at his local Employment Exchange because when asked for his previous occupation, he always answered 'Film Star'.

In Caernarfon, just as I had promised myself, I laid my socks to rest on the quayside and descended narrow stone steps to bathe my feet symbolically in the Menai Strait. The gods in my life have always been ready with a banana skin should the need arise: I slipped on some green weed and fell into the water with a splash, but grabbed at the rail and was saved from baptism by total immersion. I went further up the quayside to bathe my feet in greater safety and with more dignity. I sat there in the sunshine with the sea water cooling my sore feet, thinking that I felt fit enough to march onward to Scotland. There was an angler nearby and he looked at my resting boots and socks and said: 'Walked far?'

'From the Rhondda,' I said. 'About a hundred and fifty miles.'

He looked unimpressed, and his reel zizzed as he cast his line.

'Aye,' he said. 'It's been done before, I expect.'

CHAPTER TWO

Cymru Dreaming

My attention was drawn to a headline in the *Western Mail* and my imagination was jolted from its lazy and fruitless repose. Breathes there an inhabitant of Wales who would not be stirred to read, trumpeted in the national daily, these words: *Sahara Trek To Find Arab Tribe Who Speak Welsh.* I read it again for the flavour. *Sahara Trek To Find Arab Tribe Who Speak Welsh.* Only a few minutes before reading that I had marked down *Bishop Dies In Brothel* as my piquant headline of the week, and that had superseded the headline in a weekly paper which read *Next Claim Will Be That Jesus Christ Died For Plaid Cymru.* But this stuff about Welsh-speaking Arabs was much better. It was re-assuring. It brought the sniff of romance and the dance of sunbeams and the frap of palms to my soggy aspect of cornflakes and newspapers on this grey January day.

So: the old Welsh dream machine could still work its magic. I took the report at a gulp. A traveller was bound from Wales to Timbuktu, the town of the old slave trade deep in the blazing heart of north Africa; from there he was to penetrate the Atlas Mountains and search for a tribe of Welsh-speaking Arabs. Now, as we all know, the people in this region are mainly Berbers, but among those who are not Berbers there is a considerable mixture, a job lot of humanity blown into this corner by the breezes of history. Could there be, somewhere in some remote Atlas *cwm*, in some palmy camel-trampled El Rhondda, a long-lost tribe of Celtic Arabs who greet strangers with *sut mae** as well as *salaam el aikum*? And how, in Allah's name, in St David's name, could they have got there? The explanation, as with almost all things Celtic, is, of course, elementary. When the

* 'How are you?' 'Wotcher.'

great Celtic migration out of central Europe was under way several thousand years ago, most of the tribes settled eventually in the islands of Britain and the north-western parts of the European mainland; or they were driven there. But one group did not fancy the damp rocks of the north-west and pushed off on their own, heading for Africa to find the sunshine . . .

The lost valley, with its tribe of lost Welsh, is a potent and enduring part of Welsh wistfulness and fits quite naturally into the legends, folklore and history of a people who can look down the centuries as if down a mere staircase, who have their own private emotion called *hiraeth*, which is a kind of powerful nostalgic longing, against which a siren's song is but a televison jingle, and who have for many years travelled and settled in all the earth's imagined corners, setting up St David's societies and Cambrian clubs and other Cymrodoric columns in many strange places. Myths and legends and dreams are important property, part of the constituent of a nation's soul, and so I shall tread as nimbly as I can when discussing them.

Of course, the dream of finding the lost tribe is one that will never be realized, but that does not matter very much. In any case, it has always been much harder for Welshmen to realize their dreams than Englishmen. The English have been born with silver spoons in their mouths and so have been able to afford the achievement of their ambitions, while Welshmen, on the whole, have had to make do with wooden spoons.

It is not, however, that Welshmen have lacked the ambition and resolve to translate their dreams into reality. Consider the achievements of Hywel Dda, Hywel the Good, a king of the tenth century who dreamed of a well-ordered and law-abiding Wales, who eschewed the quarrelling that most of the princes and kinglets indulged in during those times, and determined to establish a framework of laws under which life would be more tolerable. If he did not formulate all the laws himself, Hywel was the moving force in their codification, and it is significant that he was a strong admirer of that other king who yearned for better order, and did something about it, Alfred the Great of Wessex. Hywel's

laws, the *cyfraith* Hywel, were written in Welsh and Latin
and made Wales a world leader in the establishment of a
social order. Hywel and his lawmakers had a keen eye for
detail and scrupulous fairness and Hywel believed, rather
ahead of his time, that women deserved a fairer deal under
the law. At a time when marriage in most parts of Europe
was for most women only a cut above slavery, Hywel took
the unusual step of recognizing their human rights. First of
all he took account of the fact that not all marriages could
last and recognized the seven-year-itch. So a wife who left
her man before seven years of marriage were completed had
no claim on his property, unless she could show good cause
for leaving. Hywel defined impotence and bad breath as two
of the good causes, which shows what an understanding
fellow he was. When a married couple parted, the law de-
creed that the wife should have the blankets of the marital
bed and the husband the mattress. The husband had the pig
and the wife the sheep. The husband had the hung meat and
the wife the pickled meat.

Indeed, Hywel and his lawyers thought of almost everything. For example, all the parts of the human body – well,
nearly all the parts – were given a value that could be re-
claimed if they were lost or mutilated in an assault or in an
incident where blame could be apportioned. In this grisly
part of the code, a finger was worth one cow, and a foot was
worth six cattle plus one hundred and twenty pieces of
silver. So was a nose. Also, Hywel laid down, 'the hand of
the bondsman is the same worth as the king's hand'. That
was really quite a radical statement in those days, though no
one can say if the bondsmen really believed it. The laws of
Hywel Dda tried to foresee all the eventualities of community living. If, for instance, a pig entered a house and
knocked the fire over, setting the house ablaze, and the pig
escaped, then the owner of the pig, quite rightly, was obliged
to pay compensation. 'But,' the law cautioned, 'if the swine
be burnt, then both swine and house are equal, for both are
stupid.' The perfect logic of laws like that, their straight-
forwardness, their humanity and simple justice, and their
ability to cover loopholes, made them an important advance
in men's dealings with each other. Even the role of the

humble cat in controlling vermin was recognized by law, and the following was prescribed: 'Whoever shall kill a cat that guards a house and a barn of the king . . . the cat is to be held with its head to the ground and its tail up, and then clean wheat is to be poured about it until the tip of the tail is hidden: and that is its worth.'

Hywel's laws were the framework of society in much of Wales until 1283 when the country was conquered by Edward I, annexed and made subject to English laws which, by comparison, were very dull indeed and in the long run, as we have seen, led only to the enrichment of lawyers.

Meanwhile, in 1170 or thereabouts, there was planted the seed of one of the greatest of Welsh legends, one that has ignited countless dreams and tormented the imagination of Welshmen for many centuries. The ambitious dreamer Madoc ab Owain Gwynedd, a minor noble, had wearied of the arguing that went on in his neighbourhood of north Wales. He became so fed up that he mustered ten ships and three hundred men and went off and discovered America. He thought it quite a pleasant place, with real-estate possibilities, so he sailed back to Wales to urge more Welshmen to emigrate. A second fleet set out and although Madoc and his men were never seen again the legend has it that they settled in America and lived happily ever after. It is an engaging story and was a heady fuel for dreamers, historians and explorers in the centuries that followed. In the sixteenth century various advisers in the court of Queen Elizabeth chose to believe the story on the ground that because Madoc had discovered America three centuries before the upstart Columbus, and because Madoc was Welsh, and therefore English, Spain could not justify the claims it was making on the new world. Thus did a Welsh legend become the fodder of international power politics. Increasingly the story became fashionable and Sir Walter Raleigh related it in his history of the world. During the ensuing century, as more Welsh people emigrated to America, the story gained in strength and flavour. Explorers, hunters and traders came back from their forays into the wilderness with graphic accounts of their meetings with Welsh-speaking Indians, the descendants of Madoc and his merry men. In 1686, Morgan

Jones, a preacher who had been a student at Jesus College, Oxford, and whose honesty therefore cannot be questioned, reported that seventeen years earlier he had been captured by Indians in what is now South Carolina. As the Indians were about to put him to death, Morgan Jones cried out in Welsh: 'So it's curtains for me then, boys bach!' Or words to that effect. Some of the Indians, recognizing the language of heaven, called off the execution in the nick of time and took Morgan Jones away to live with them. They confirmed that they were descended from a Welshman who had come across the ocean from the east, countless moons before, Morgan Jones said that he stayed with the Indians for four months and preached to them in Welsh three times a week.

A tale like this, along with fresh stories emerging from the frontier regions of trappers and guides meeting fair-skinned and blue-eyed Indians, heaped a fair fire to keep the legend bubbling. No doubt those who told the stories liked to tell their listeners exactly what they wanted to hear – and the listeners wanted to be told tales that would match the jig of their hopes and imaginations.

The romance of the Welsh Indians gripped the minds of a group of Welsh literati living in London who had formed a society called the Gwyneddigion. One of the members was Iolo Morganwg, the poet and embellisher of legends. At one time he wanted to lead an expedition to hunt for the Indians – particularly after the arrival in Britain of a Cherokee chieftain, who had taken the name of William Bowles, and who said yes, the Welsh Indians really existed. In the end, however, it was John Thomas Evans, son of a Methodist minister, who left his native Caernarfonshire, backed by the Gwyneddigion, determined to get to the bottom of the story. He left in 1792, aged twenty-two; and when you consider the rough conditions of travel over the sea and land in those days, the nature of the territory he planned to enter, the absence of maps and the perils of disease, it was an epic undertaking. It was at least as epic as the journey of another Welshman, H. M. Stanley, who, in the next century, sought, not Indians, but Dr Livingstone. John Evans started out from Baltimore, crossed to the Ohio river, followed it for five hundred miles to the Mississippi, and then to St Louis.

Big Chief Ianto Two Rivers him say 'We hammer Custer's team twenty points to nil!'

By now he was in territory held by Spain and the local governor, clearly a man of scant imagination, did not believe the Welshman's story and kept him in prison for two years in the belief that he was a British secret agent. Evans was only unlocked when a fellow Welshman, one Jones, heard of his plight and interceded on his behalf. Now John Evans joined up with an expedition, led by a Scot, which was to explore the Missouri valley with the aim of securing trading rights and strengthening Spain's claim to the land. There was also the hope that the explorers would find a pass through the mountains to the Pacific Ocean. They set off up the Missouri and were forced to stop when hard weather set in and passed the winter with a tribe of friendly Indians. When the warmer weather came John Evans was sent on up the river with a small party, and once more he wintered with

Indians, giving them gifts of flags from the King of Spain. When at last he decided to turn back he had explored the upper Missouri almost to the Canadian border. This was seven years before the famous journey of Daniel Clark and Meriwether Lewis, who did find a route through the mountains to the Pacific and have all the glory in the history books. And with them they had the well-drawn map made by the young Welshman who had searched for Welsh Indians. As for John Evans, he heard not a single word of Welsh in his long brave trek, save his own prayers. His journey lasted more than two years, and two years after his return from the wilderness he died in New Orleans. In the next century there was another attempt to find Madoc's children. A group of Welsh-Americans financed an expedition by two men who made a long and fruitless search of the Missouri. And even when America had been thoroughly explored, the legend would not lie still. In 1953 the Daughters of the American Revolution erected a marker near Mobile in Alabama. It reads: 'In memory of Prince Madoc, who landed on the shores of Mobile Bay in 1170 and left behind, with the Indians, the Welsh language.'

The dream of Sam Roberts of Llanbrynmair was to found a Welsh colony on land he bought in Tennessee. Two parties of Welsh people settled on the land, but quite soon the dream disintegrated in disillusion. The civil war started and the luckless Welsh happened to be sandwiched between the opposing sides. What with that and their considerable financial difficulties the people started to stream away.

The settlement of Patagonia was another great Welsh dream and adventure. Welshmen sought refuge from the oppression of landlords and poverty in their native land by founding a colony in that far-off stretch of South America. In 1865, at the time the Sam Roberts settlement was crumbling in Tennessee, one hundred and fifty-three people, from Mountain Ash, from Ffestiniog, Aberdare, Rhosllanerchrugog – and Wigan – assembled on the quay at Liverpool to commit themselves to the dream of a New Wales in a land at the earth's end. They boarded the converted clipper *Mimosa* and hoisted the flag of the Red Dragon and sang a touching song, especially composed, about their

home-to-be which would have a Welshman on the throne.
With them they had bundles of pound notes and ten shilling
notes, printed in Welsh, because they and their backers
imagined that they were off to rich valleys in the garden of
Eden. What they found, however, was an allotment in hell.
In the early years they knew hunger, thirst and desolation, a
cruel dashing of their hopes. Some lost heart, but slowly the
pioneers built their colony and their democracy, albeit
under Argentinian jurisdiction. They built their chapels and
Welsh schools and founded their newspaper. Their senate
was elected annually and both men and women had the vote
at eighteen. They tamed the land and grew wheat and raised
sheep. They endured floods and the threat of attack by
Indians and one or two of them died in gunfights with
bandits. People continued to emigrate from Wales to Patagonia until 1912, and the story of the Pampas Welsh rates
as an epic chapter in man's pursuit of dreams. For a while
they had their free Wales overseas, their Welsh-speaking
democracy, and it was all done without enslaving or killing
other human beings. The old dream, though, has crumbled
somewhat. Increasingly, Patagonia was settled by immigrants from other countries, was absorbed more fully into
Argentina, and Welsh was replaced by Spanish as the first
language. For many years one of the schools educated its
pupils trilingually: they emerged speaking Spanish, Welsh
and English. Today, however, the accent is firmly on Spanish and while the older people cling to Welsh and Welsh
customs, the language is not spoken by many of the young
and is fading away. There is a certain piquancy about the
old Welsh place names mixed up with all the Spanish names;
and a piquancy, too, about the names of the people: Miguel
Jones and Pedro Roberts, and so on. One August, at the
National Eisteddfod of Wales, I met Rene Griffiths, a
young Patagonian with a lively guitar and a poppy poncho.
He had hardly any English because he was brought up in
Spanish and Welsh, and he was talking in Welsh with a visiting American girl who had been taught the language by her
grandmother. The girl was a rarity. The Welsh, when they
emigrated, hardly ever passed on their language to their children. About one hundred thousand Welsh people sought a

better existence overseas during the nineteenth and early twentieth centuries, many of them to America. They had to struggle in new lands and either saw no point in keeping alive the old language, or found it too difficult to do so, and so it withered very quickly. Unlike the Scots and the Irish, who managed to keep a hold on some fragments of their identity for a long time in north America and elsewhere, the Welsh, once their language had gone, were made naked and were more rapidly assimilated.

Of quite a different character, as dreams go, was the dream of Welsh whisky. This cause – either noble or damnable depending upon your point of view – was pursued by the colourful and eccentric Squire Richard Lloyd Price. He lived at Rhiwlas, a magnificent house and estate near Bala in Merioneth. He was a man of broad vision, a man with an eye for style who would do nothing by halves. So that when he conceived the idea of Welsh whisky he built a huge distillery at Frongoch, on the banks of the Tryweryn river, whose waters are bright and pure. From Scotland he imported Scotch experts to give advice, and the work began. But he soon ran into difficulties because some of the local farmers felt it was wrong to sell their barley in secret and regretfully bumped up their prices and profits accordingly . . . you know how it is.

When the whisky at last went on the market it was advertised as 'the mingled souls of peat and barley washed white within the waters of Tryweryn and may claim to paint landscapes on the brain of man'. Unfortunately, and for all that inspired copywriting, the landscapes on the brains of men fell rather short of being Constables or Van Goghs. By all accounts – and, of course, it is now unlikely that there would be a Welsh whisky drinker alive today, to tell the tale – the whisky did not improve with age. It grew worse by the day. It tasted awful. The Prince of Wales was given a bottle of this *hwtch Cymreig* when he visited Bala in 1894. Sensibly, he did not open it and kept it in the cellars at Windsor. Eighty years later, unexploded, the bottle was sent back home to Wales and is now in the national museum. To the delight of the temperance movement (whose own dream of a sober province was not to be realized) the distillery closed

down just before the First World War. The whisky dream
had cost Squire Price a lot of money and he ran into serious
financial trouble, saving himself only by putting his shirt on a
horse in the Cambridgeshire which, fortunately, won. The
squire's debt to the beast is remembered in the epitaph he
asked to have carved over the family vault near Bala: 'I
bless the good horse Bendigo/Who built this tomb for me.'
That might have been the end of Welsh whisky, but the
Welsh dream machine still chuffs its magic smoke and
infects imaginations ... now two men are planning to
make a second attempt to manufacture a drinkable Welsh
whisky. But surely they won't call it whisky: that name
belongs to Scotch; and whiskey is the Irish potation. I think
they will have to be completely ethnic, spell it in accordance
with Welsh orthography, and call it *wisci*; and if they need a
brand-name what could be better than Squire Price? How
long will it be before saloon bars ring to the cry of 'Landlord, a double Welsh on the rocks for my journalist friend!'

One of the more enchanting Welsh dreams was that
dreamed by Bob Hydraulic. He once worked out a complex
scheme to construct a large cantilevered and hydraulic-
powered moon – hence his nickname – over the harbour at
Holyhead, for the delight of visitors. Unfortunately, this
moon has yet to rise.

Many a Welsh dream has focused on gold. Men have
grubbed and panned and tunnelled for it in the hills near
Dolgellau, in Merioneth, and around Dolaucothi, in Carmarthenshire, for many years. Considering the number of
people who hurried to these districts in the latter part of the
last century, in the hope of striking it rich, it is reasonable to
talk of a Welsh gold rush. But nobody made a fortune and
the gold quest, for the great majority of Welsh fortyniners,
ended in empty pockets, housemaid's knee, the foundations
of arthritis and a lifelong antipathy towards rainbows. The
fact is that although gold mining was a commercial proposi-
tion for a while, the Romans had beaten everyone to it long
before. They used British slave labour and sophisticated
technology, opencast and shaft mining and water sluices to
wash the rock away, and sent off heaps of gold to the im-
perial mints at Lyons and Rome. It seems likely, indeed,

that Welsh gold was one of the main reasons for the Roman invasion of the British island. Today, some multi-national mining groups still hanker for an opportunity to dig for the gold that the Romans left behind, but the environmental interests have so far succeeded in keeping them off the grass. There is just enough Welsh gold left, however, to fashion into Royal wedding rings and to keep bright the embers of the dreams of the handful of people who still go hunting for it.

Not all Welsh dreams go unrewarded. In the 1920s Welshmen crouched beside their wireless apparatus and with the aid of crystal and cat's whisker heard crackling *Cymraeg*, and began to dream of a wireless service for the Welsh language. The letters they wrote to newspapers urging this bold step were remarkably similar to the ones their sons and grandsons wrote fifty years on. Now a radio service for Welsh-speakers is being created; so is a television for all Wales, for Welsh-speakers and non-Welsh-speakers alike. Radio and television play a considerable part in the health of the Welsh language and we should bear in mind that when those crystal-set listeners started agitating for more Welsh there were nine hundred thousand Welsh-speakers. Now there are fewer than six hundred thousand, and pessimists fear that by the time a satisfactory Welsh language television service is on the air the entire audience will be able to crowd around one set.

In other important fields, dreams have been translated into the reality of bricks and mortar. I have written earlier in this book of the patriots who were part of a new mood of national awareness, recognized the perils that menaced Welsh culture and national identity, and set out to found the university, the *eisteddfod*, the museum and library. They were taking up the thread of the dream of Owain Glyndwr who waged a war of independence against England in the first eight years of the fifteenth century. Glyndwr was a hero, an educated and cultured man who retrieved all of Wales through his generalship, then revealed his statesmanship and vision. He called parliaments, set up courts, appointed bishops, dispatched ambassadors to foreign courts, began to free the Welsh church from English influence and planned universities, one in the north and one in the south. But Glyndwr was ahead of his time – that was his tragedy – and his days were numbered. The English crushed the rebellion, repudiated Glyndwr's UDI and smashed the dream of a free Wales. Glyndwr, outlawed and a broken man, faded from the scene, to be rediscovered, refurbished and regilded as a great Welsh hero, and slotted into the Welsh dream, and hagiology, by historians and storytellers in the nineteenth and twentieth centuries. Glyndwr's ideas about a university took five more centuries to mature into reality; if there is one lesson the Welsh have learned it is that there is no such thing as overnight success. The university movement began in earnest during the 1840s and struggled against hostility, indifference and chronic money shortage. An important factor in the survival of the dream was the support of many thousands of ordinary people. Contributions – pennies and sixpences – poured in from education-conscious miners in the south and quarrymen in the north. The first college was founded, in Aberystwyth, quite by chance when a property tycoon went bankrupt after building a turreted Ruritanian castle of a hotel on the promenade. The hotel was offered for £15,000 and the college pioneers scraped together the deposit. In October 1872 the first students, twenty-six of them, arrived to start their degree courses. The college lurched from crisis to crisis. There was a severe fire, an embarrassing lack of funds, a strong move to have it closed down, and government indifference to the whole venture. But at last, in 1893, the University of Wales, with colleges in Aberystwyth, Bangor and Cardiff, and with the right to grant its own degrees, was given a charter and allowed in from the cold. A historian described it as 'the peasants' university' but it enshrined a long-held Welsh ideal and ambition. In his history of University College, Aberystwyth, Dr E. L. Ellis wrote: 'Without much help from the educated and well-off, the Welsh people had risen to create a more or less complete system of education depending on the support of the mass of the people. Herein lay its rarity.'

Those Welshmen who have dreamed of playing a more important part in the management of their own affairs, in the fields of government and administration, have had to wait a while. In 1910 Keir Hardie urged the appointment of a secretary of state for Welsh affairs and the establishment of a Welsh Office; and, lo, fifty-four years later it came to pass. Welsh people have been debating the idea of a Welsh parliament or assembly on and off for more than eighty years. Now they are close to getting it.

Many years ago the Labour politician Arthur Henderson said that, given home rule, Wales would be a utopia. Certainly a compound Welsh dream would include home rule; and also a hydraulic moon shining over Holyhead harbour; an endless supply of oil from the Celtic Sea; an end to coal mining; perfect television reception in every *cwm* and cranny; the writing of the great Welsh novel – against which the writing of the great American novel would seem like the dashing-off of a pulp western; the completion of the Cardiff to Merthyr Tydfil trunk road – the main cause of premature balding and ageing among Welsh drivers for nigh on fifty years; the discovery of a mighty gold reef at Dolgellau; a bilingual citizenry from Flat Holm to the Skerries; the trebling or quadrupling of the seating capacity of the national rugby stadium in Cardiff; the truth at last about that Welsh try against New Zealand in 1905; Lloyd George's second coming; the establishment of a Welsh whisky industry; the finding of enormous laverbread deposits on the Welsh coast, coinciding with a sudden world demand for it; the re-peopling of the countryside; the declaration of a public holiday every time Wales score more than twenty points; the development of an aerosol spray to combat thieving valleys sheep; the compulsory retirement of committee chairmen after forty years in the chair, or on their hundredth birthday, whichever is sooner; another great religious revival to pack the chapels; the development of vineyards on sunny hillsides; the endowing of a chair of rugby at the University of Wales; the erection of an opera house and theatre complex in Cardiff; Welsh seats in the great councils of Europe and the world – and the astonishing discovery, in a lost valley in a remote district of America, of the Welsh-speaking Indians descended from Madoc ab Owain Gwynedd.

Even as my pen squeaks across the page there are some astronomers and science writers talking on my radio in the background, agreeing that the universe is so large, and no doubt infinite, that there is a mathematical probability that, somewhere among all those teeming stars, there is a planet exactly the same as our own foolish Earth. Perhaps, someone speculates, it has the same problems, democracies, tyrannies, cultures and languages.

The idea sets my thoughts racing: is there another Wales? Before I can stop my imagination's crazy progress I visualize a time when inter-galactic travel is a commonplace and there are telescopes that enable us to look beyond belief and fuels that enable us to keep neck-and-neck with light itself. I now see men, imbued with the spirit of brave John Evans who searched for Welsh-speakers in the American wilderness, walking towards their space craft at the Aberporth launching base. The bold Welsh astronauts, or *startrecwyr* as we call them, shut the hatches and I hear the breath-bating countdown ... '*deg, naw, wyth, saith, chwech, pump, pedwar, tri, dau, un* ... lift-off!' And the good ship Madoc rises to find Welsh among the stars.

CHAPTER THREE

The Greatest Show on Earth

There are five phenomena of migration which have fascinated and baffled all students of the behaviour of the world's creatures for many years. There is the long journey of the salmon, thrusting his way to his spawning ground, hurling himself in defiance of gravity and exhaustion past all obstacles: there is the wonderful migration of birds over vast distances, though storms and weariness decimate their numbers; there is the autumn journey of the freshwater eels who cross the Atlantic to breed and to die in the tendrilled tenebrous swells of the Sargasso sea; there is the bizarre swarming of Arctic lemmings and their mass leap to doom like jilted swains; and there is the curious journeying of Welshmen who, responding to primeval urge, head each August for the national *eisteddfod* of Wales, an institution which has, to greater or lesser degree, the characteristics of an opium den, a chapel, a big top, a prom, a soirée, a saloon bar, a cocktail bar, a plotters' bar, a rain dance, a literary meeting, a political meeting, a human sacrifice, a picnic, a pavement café, a bookshop, a durbar, a debate, a high table, a bird table, a mudbath, a maypole jig, a cricket pavilion, a theatre, a fête, a marriage bureau, a rugby dinner, a harvest dinner, a family reunion, a regimental reunion, a village square, a market day, a boardroom and a hoedown.

To be a part of all that goes on in and around this magic compound, Welshmen, nearly-Welshmen and descendants of Welshmen will shut their homes and offices, down tools and postpone business deals, honeymoons and dying. They will journey from Punta Arenas, Paris, Patagonia and Pwllheli, from Lime Springs, Alice Springs, Palm Springs and Llanwrtyd Wells, from Red River and Red Roses. They will come by jet and car, and, if necessary, on crutches.

There are some Welshmen whose pulses quicken on New Year's Eve, not because of the wine, or the prospect of a clasp beneath the mistletoe; but because, with the old year wrung out and the new year rung in, it seems like downhill all the way to the first week in August and the greatest show on earth. 'To think of it,' these mainliners muse happily on New Year's dawn, 'only two hundred and fourteen days to the next national *eisteddfod*.' There are some who, in a manner reminiscent of the Chinese custom of calling the years the Year of the Wolf, or the Year of the Horse, and so on, tend to reckon the passage of time in terms of national *eisteddfodau* and the towns where they were held: the Year of Bangor, the Year of Carmarthen, the Year of Llanelli. There are some who fervently hope that, when they have witnessed their last sunset, they will find that eternity is a great *eisteddfod* in the sky: entered through the pearly turn-stiles.

To an outsider the *Royal National Eisteddfod*, patron H.M. the Queen, is a mystery, a folkloric fog into which a portion of the Welsh nation disappears, making strange sounds; something to do with druids in long gowns, and with poems and singing and swords and flowers, all enveloped in a bubble-bath of Welsh. To others the whole business is akin to a pain in the neck. More than a century ago *The Times* thundered irascibly that the national *eisteddfod* was 'a mischievous and selfish piece of sentimentalism, simply a foolish interference with the natural progress of civilization and prosperity. It is monstrous folly to encourage the Welsh in a loving fondness for their old language.' The *Daily Telegraph*, in the same vein, called the festival 'a national debauch of sentimentality'. And *The Times*, again, grumbled colonially that the *eisteddfod* housed 'practices tolerated and even cherished which would be put down in England.'

Some people would agree with those Victorian judgements even today. But critics of the *eisteddfod* sometimes seem a po-faced lot. To understand it you must retain your sense of humour; you must take the beast seriously enough, but never make the mistake of taking it too seriously. And there can be no reasonable understanding of Wales without some knowledge of its anatomy. So let us take our scalpels and rummage around.

The national *eisteddfod* is unique. It is a sort of annual general meeting of Welsh Wales, in one sense a stockade into which people can retreat and bolt the gates against English, in another sense it is an open house for all of Wales, the embodiment of hope, the vehicle of tradition and dreams, an assertion of collective personality, an exhibition, a major culture festival. It is a most necessary institution, a generator, a defence, a water-hole.

The national is the largest and most important of a network of *eisteddfodau*. Villages, towns, chapels, schools, counties, miners, young farmers, students, the Welsh youth movement and even old age pensioners, have their own *eisteddfodau*. All these festivals have their spiritual roots in the bardic sessions – *eisteddfod* means session – that were known in Wales at least a thousand years ago. There are records of a famous *eisteddfod* held in Cardigan town in 1176 and it was fitting that the 1976 national should go to the town, exactly eight hundred years later. Then, as now, the bards met to read their poetry and prose to each other, to vie with each other in the composition of witty verse, and to play the harp in competition. The harp was always preferred to the bagpipes in Wales, and eight centuries ago a poet wrote:

> The churl did blow a grating shriek,
> The bag did swell, and harshly squeak,
> As does a goose from nightmare crying,
> Or dog crushed by a chest when dying.

The bards in old Wales had prestige, which is not to say that they do not have prestige in new Wales. But in old Wales, they were always more than poets; they were the historians in their communities, the genealogists, tutors, storytellers, gossips and entertainers. They were patronized by the princes, kinglets and well-to-do, and all the best families had their own private bard. They wrote to order: a poem to celebrate a victory in battle, verses on the birth of a son, words on a girl's beauty, ditties poking fun, rhymes about successful hunts. In the laws of Hywel Dda, in the tenth century, royal bards ranked eighth among the officers of the state and had grace and favour houses and free land. Moreover, they were valued at one hundred and twenty-six cows and anyone who insulted them could be fined six cows and twenty silver pence. Freelance or wandering bards sang for their suppers. They called at big houses and sang and recited in exchange for pot luck and palliasse. From the twelfth century to the fifteenth the bards created for Wales a literary and musical reputation on a European scale and some of their work is read and enjoyed today.

The bardic traditions and way of life fell into decline after the defeat of Owain Glyndwr in the fifteenth century, partly because the English suspected the poets of being stirrers of trouble and rebellious feeling; partly because of the decline of patronage; but a thin thread was maintained. The romance of the bards and their surviving works had a profound effect on a key figure in the story of the *eisteddfod*, one Edward Williams, alias Iolo Morganwg, who lived from 1747 to 1826. He illuminated the cultural life of Wales, and of London, with his scholarship, his talk and his writing. He passionately desired to see bardism restored to its former glory, and he also hankered for the kind of rituals that he imagined the druids of ancient Britain had indulged in. He was also devoted to his native county of Glamorgan and sought to glorify it by showing that the medieval poet Dafydd ap Gwilym had written in glowing terms about it and had been, indeed, a Glamorgan boy.

Iolo was a dreamer and his passions led him to invention. I shrink from using such a word as liar in relation to old Iolo; it is much too harsh for a man whose fabricated stories, 'supported' by ancient manuscripts, were really quite harmless and which, in the end, served a most useful purpose. He had the gift of telling people what they wanted to hear and he span such fascinating tales that everyone believed him. Iolo was a great walker as well as a great talker and he was a familiar sight in the countryside, a short man with grey hair over his collar, dressed in a blue coat and corduroy trousers (or 'nether integuments' as one Victorian author described them). Iolo read a book as he walked, through spectacles perched on the end of his nose. He was a considerable eccentric – at one time he decided that if cattle and sheep could live off grass, men could also; and he and a similarly eccentric friend spent a day on their hands and knees grazing a field. But at sunset they felt ravenous and hurried off for bread and cheese. On another occasion Iolo planned to go to America to hunt for Welsh-speaking Indians and went into training by sleeping out rough in the countryside. But he became so cold, wet and stiff that he abandoned the project.

Iolo's triumph of invention was the *Gorsedd Beirdd Ynys Prydain*, or Assembly of the Bards of the Island of Britain. It is now an established part of the *eisteddfod* and it was Iolo the Fib who grafted it on. The *gorsedd* is a sort of guild of literati and it provides at 'the national' the ceremonial aspect, the incantations, the robes of white, blue and green, the dancing elves, the sword of peace, the horn of plenty, the sheaf of corn. Iolo perpetrated his splendid fraud at the Ivy Bush Hotel in Carmarthen in 1819 where he was impresario at a three-day *eisteddfod*. The winning poet was invested with a ribbon as he sat in a large chair; and on the last day Iolo admitted a number of people to his new bardic order, handing out ribbons of white, blue and green which, he said, were the ancient insignia of bardism. He also strewed a circle of pebbles on the ground to represent the sacred *gorsedd* stones. Today the stones are substantial rocks and they stand all over Wales, wherever a national *eisteddfod* has been staged, like miniature Stonehenges. When the national got under way as an institution in the 1860s, the *gorsedd* of bards assumed a prominent role in it. Some time later Wales learned the truth about Iolo. The *gorsedd*'s position as a cuckoo in the *eisteddfod* nest was exposed. But by then the *gorsedd* was firmly entrenched in Welsh life, and for a simple reason. All the tribes of the world like ritual, badges, medals, strange hats, parades and archaic nomenclature and language. If you were to apply hard logic and harder accountancy to many of the ceremonies and other frills that decorate human existence they could not be justified. But people want them. Englishmen, and Welshmen too, titter to see the bardic rituals, yet see nothing wrong with people

dressing in feathers and black stockings for Garter ceremonies. Indeed, Englishmen strip off readily to dress up like
court cards, and town councillors everywhere have an ambition to be a mayor, a preening panjandrum in a tricorn
hat. No, Wales needs its own pageantry and peacockery,
even if it has been cooked up, and the *gorsedd* provides it.
Almost all ceremonial comes within a whisker of being hilarious, and the Welsh kind is no better or worse than any
other. The *gorsedd* also fulfils another function: it provides
an honours system. You can enter the *gorsedd* by passing its
literature and music examinations, but you can also be admitted as an honorary member for distinguished service to
Welsh life and culture. And it is an honour that counts for
something.

So Iolo's masterpiece of imagination – don't you agree
that it would be unfair to call him a liar, even a fabricator? –
lives on; and Iolo himself, though his runaway imagination
has been expressed, has no stain upon his character, because
his heart was in the right place: in Wales. In 1974, when the
national *eisteddfod* was held at Carmarthen, Iolo was half-
canonized. A stained-glass window to his memory, and to
his *eisteddfod* of 1819, was unveiled in the lounge bar of the
Ivy Bush Hotel. Who but the Welsh would erect, in a bar, a
stained-glass window in memory of a lovable faker and
poet?

Iolo would certainly approve of the way that the national
eisteddfod has developed. It is an important, serious cultural
festival, with a strong competitive element, a centre for orchestras, soloists, bands, choirs, poets, dancers and artists in
wood, stone, paint and metal. Tickets for the major events
are booked a year in advance and the festival is an exhibition of some of the richness and variety of the Welsh
language. Its function as a meeting-place, as a holiday, a
talking-shop, is also a part of the essence of it. The *eisteddfod*
is a sort of Welsh Simla, and so it was not surprising that in
1974 the Secretary of State for Wales, complete with senior
staff and red dispatch boxes, moved to the *eisteddfod* for a
while and set up a field headquarters there.

The fact that the language of the *eisteddfod* is Welsh does
not make it off-limits to people who do not know Welsh.

After all, much of it – the music and arts and crafts is language-less – and a lot of the Welsh-language singing may be appreciated without knowledge of the language. Moreover, HTV, the commercial television company, lends out small hand-held receivers which pick up an English commentary on what is going on and you see them in use all the time. The question of the Welsh-only *eisteddfod* is a controversy renewed at regular intervals when a case is put for allowing English back on to the *eisteddfod* stage and into adjudications. The argument is that this would enable all the people of Wales to play a fuller part in the national festival, that the mingling of the two languages would create greater understanding and unity, the Welsh-speakers are making a mistake by withdrawing into their August laager because they are missing an opportunity to build bridges out to English-speakers. Well, there was a time when English had a part to play in the event, and the Welsh-only rule was stiffened in 1950 because people felt that English might, in the long run, shoulder Welsh aside; they felt that there should be a deep and pure well of Welsh to draw from. I am not at all convinced that if the *eisteddfod* were bilingual, or if there were an English day or two, that people from the non-Welsh-speaking areas would trek in their thousands to go there. They might have once, but times have changed. In any case, people who do not have Welsh are not excluded; they are welcome. A lot of English-only people take part in it as musicians, or as singers who have learned Welsh songs in the same way that they learn Italian and French songs. There is also the character and function of the *eisteddfod* to consider; it is in one sense a festival of Wales, but it is also a festival, a celebration, of the Welsh language, and there is no reason why English-speakers should not enjoy it at that level. And large numbers of them do enjoy it and support it. I do not believe that the Welsh-only rule will be changed; to do so, in my opinion, would be to water the wine. Sometimes local authorities in Wales withdraw grants from the national *eisteddfod* – they are permitted to give it money under an Act of Parliament of 1959 – as a mark of their displeasure at the all-Welsh rule. The bigotry of the councillors is in sharp contrast to the welcome and support that the *eisteddfod* receives from ordinary people when it sets up its mighty camp in anglicized areas.

The *eisteddfod* receives about a fifth of its money from local authorities. Much of the rest comes from appeals and fund-raising by volunteers. Every year, with quite touching faith, they set out to raise the cash by holding dances and sales and by passing round the hat to individuals, and industry as well as councils. So far they have succeeded – proof enough that goodwill for the *eisteddfod* is deeply rooted and that Welsh really is the language of heaven. But the question of money has grown increasingly acute. The prospect of the *eisteddfod* costing a quarter of a million pounds to stage has become a realistic fear. The festival needs financial advisers as much as it needs poets; the muse and mammon must sit at the same table. In the nineteen-sixties and seventies towns and districts no longer clamoured, as they did once, for the honour of having 'the national' in their area because they were anxious about raising the money.

The *eisteddfod* is peripatetic, held in north Wales one year, and south Wales the next, so that the Welshness can be sprinkled around evenly like fertilizer. The transporting of all the buildings is the largest removal operation in Britain and it takes the best part of a year to get them all dismantled, transported to the other end of the country – Wales is two hundred miles from top to bottom – and re-erected. Prime among the buildings is the great pavilion, a stately pleasure prefab with a hot tin roof and seats for eight thousand people; a sort of Welsh Albert Hall on wheels. It is nearly two hundred and fifty feet long, steel-framed and wood-panelled, with a large, always floriated, stage, and dressing rooms, kitchens and offices behind it. There is also a press centre where reporters tap out their reports, telephone them to Cardiff, Liverpool, London and other newspaper centres, and laugh at each other's rotten jokes. Once I nearly killed a man in this room at the *eisteddfod*. He was sitting quietly, eating his snack lunch and drinking tea on one of the press tables which consist of boards placed loosely across trestles. I entered the room and sat down on the other end of the table, creating a seesaw effect that projected his refreshment across the room like missiles from a siege catapult, and just missed giving him a dreadful uppercut to the jaw. I was a little depressed by my own clumsiness but was considerably cheered a little later to observe two fame-encrusted *eisteddfod* figures slip on the fudgy mud, without which an *eisteddfod* would not be complete, and

Couldn't get Gareth Edwards then could you?

roll down an incline, gathering a coating of mud like confectionery bars going through a chocolate dip.

Journalists, of course, like an *eisteddfod* to produce a lot of news and, if possible, a controversy or two. They are rarely disappointed. A great show like this, run by Welsh people for Welsh people, can hardly please all the people all of the time, and the *eisteddfod* turns up plenty of individuals, groups and official bodies who complain about some aspect of it. Over the years it has been suggested to me several times that I ought to expose the awful truth about the *eisteddfod*, but no one seems able to say what that awful truth is. Controversy and dark hints are as old as the *eisteddfod*, and are a part of the fun and the mustard. For sub-editors, who have to write the headlines in newspapers, *eisteddfod*, being a ten-letter word, is something of a problem. They like '*steddfod* for short, '*fod* for shorter, and write headlines saying things like BARDS IN FOD SHOCK. A row can be guaranteed when someone like a president-of-the-day makes a speech on the *eisteddfod* stage which is reckoned to be political. Such speeches have been made at the *eisteddfod* for many years, and Lloyd George made them frequently, but today they always cause trouble and those councillors who recognize the dangers of free speech threaten to cut off the *eisteddfod*'s grant as a reprisal. Although criticism and discontent are part of the national *eisteddfod*, it rolls on majestically. The number of people who can speak Welsh is falling, but the attendances at 'the national' have been increasing, an indication of the value that people place upon it. Even the young *graffiti* artists approve. In the manner of football fans who daub slogans saying Arsenal Rule OK or Liverpool Rule OK, Welsh *graffitists* scrawled on rocks near Carmarthen: Eisteddfod Rule OK.

When all is said, it is an event which creates fun. A lot of people do not visit the pavilion at all; they are content to amble round *y maes*, the field, meeting friends and acquaintances and relatives, swapping the eternal password: and conversation opener:

'*Yma am yr wythnos?*'

'Here for the week?'

The festival is a dry one: no alcohol, in keeping with the old Welsh nonconformist tradition. It is a week of Sundays. Off the field, however, in the hotels and public houses nearby, it is a week of Saturday nights, of singing, gossiping, drinking. The *eisteddfod* is a kind of washing machine into which the Welsh toss their psyches to be scrubbed and dried ready for another year's battling.

As I remarked earlier, 'the national' is at the top of a great *eisteddfodic* pyramid. There are scores of smaller events where competition is at least as fierce and where there is just as much enjoyment. Some are all-Welsh, some are bilingual, depending upon the district. In many villages an *eisteddfod* is considered to be less than successful if it finishes early, and people get pleasure in recalling, and boasting: 'Ah, the 1973 one ... finished at three in the morning.' And, of course, the smaller *eisteddfodau* are a great proving-ground for aspiring writers, poets, musicians and singers whose ambition is to be a national winner.

One of the most famous festivals on the *eisteddfod* circuit is the one held each May in the village of Pontrhydfendigaid in Cardiganshire. Its money prizes are the largest in Wales, and it is one of the richest *eisteddfodau*, because it was set up and endowed by the philanthropist and local-boy-made-money, Sir David James. He wanted a living and lively and happy memorial, as well as the great sombre tomb, black as coal, that was built for him down the road at Strata Florida. So he founded the *eisteddfod* in the village, funded it with two hundred thousand pounds, plus forty-five thousand pounds for a pavilion seating three thousand people. With prizes of up to six hundred pounds for the winners of some events, Pontrhydfendigaid *eisteddfod* is not to be passed lightly by. The singers, choirs, poets, reciters, music soloists and orchestras come flocking. It would please Sir David, who was a bit of an impresario like Iolo Morganwg, because a lot of people are getting a lot of fun out of the money he left and the event he started.

Trophies are an important part of any *eisteddfod*. Competition has been intrinsic since bards first met many centuries ago. In some parts of the world you may know a man's prowess by the number of his cattle, or his gold bars, his divorces, his camels, the feathers in his bonnet, his wives, his concubines. In Wales it is caps and chairs. The caps go to rugby footballers and the chairs to poets. For in a land where warriors and bards have been fêted equally for a

dozen centuries, a breathtaking verse is acclaimed as much
as a match-winning drop goal. By tradition the poet who
wins at an *eisteddfod* gets a fitting and noble prize, a high-
backed, carved oaken throne that friends and descendants
may admire, a glory that only time and woodworm can
erase. Today this kind of carved throne is rarer, and the soft
modern easy chair is more often the poet's prize.

Still, many a man has partly furnished his home through
his rhymer's craft. Some poets own thirty or forty of them.
But no one comes near Mr Carellio Morgan – Carellio
means lover of light – who lives near Aberystwyth, and who
had, at the last count, won a hundred and ten chairs. He is
the undisputed Chairman Mawr* of Wales. In his home
there is room for no more than thirty chairs and he has given
the rest to friends and chapels. When we talked he sat in the
chair he won at a Strata Florida *eisteddfod* and I sat in one
he took at Tregaron. 'As a young man I was a boxer, and
poetry is very much like boxing,' he said to me. 'You have to
perfect your technique and know the skills and the weaknesses of your opponents and you have to find the right
words that will land like good punches and win the prizes.
Competition in poetry can be fierce; we poets have our pride
and our jealousy. I have never stood on life's touchlines and
I have always gone out to win and to compose poetry built
to last.'

Compared with the way that the work of poets sells in
English, the work of Welsh poets sells well. An English poet
might sell a thousand copies of his work in England. A
Welsh poet might sell the same number – but the English-
speaking population of Britain is fifty-five million; and the
Welsh-speaking population is half a million.

Welsh poets write a lot about the countryside and its
creatures, the neighbourhoods where they made their first
footprints, the girls they courted and those they loved hope-
lessly from afar. It would be nice, though, if one or two of
them could write some verses in praise of food, their native
dishes, for the *eisteddfod* needs to turn its attention rather
more towards what its patrons eat. Welshmen are a little
philistine about food, and Welsh cooking, which is essen-

* *Mawr* – great or big.

tially simple and pastoral, like French provincial cooking, has been neglected. As a showcase for good Welsh things the festival should also offer good Welsh food. There should be *cawl* kitchens perhaps – *cawl* is a delicious meat and vegetable broth – serving cheap and sustaining meals. And where is the *bara brith*, the fruit loaf that Mother used to make, and the *cacen gri*, the thin baked griddle cake that was one of the routes to Lloyd George's heart. It would be no bad thing if the *eisteddfod* organizers thought about giving people the taste of Wales as well as the musical and poetic sound of it.

Of course, not all of the thousands of people who squeeze into the great pavilion at the national *eisteddfod* for the chairing or the crowning of the champion bard have an abiding interest in poetry, nor will they all read the winning work. But they would not miss the fêting of the hero. It says much about Wales that people will gather like this for the magic moment when the winning poet, whose identity has been hidden by a *ffug enw*, or nom-de-pome, is called and stands revealed in the blaze of television lights. Called forward by blaring trumpets, led by a man dressed like a Saracen, he ascends to his chair and sits, the aureate laureate, to be acclaimed by the multitude . . . before he is fed to the jostling wolves of the press.

One year the BBC in London broadcast a special report on this emotional moment when the winning bard revealed himself to the throng. And the reporter made one of those splendidly irretrievable slips of the tongue. 'Then, to loud applause from the crowd of ten thousand people,' the reporter said to listening Britain, 'the winning poet stood up to relieve himself.'

CHAPTER FOUR

The Talk of the Land

Once upon a time, in Aberystwyth, a gentleman entered a tobacconist's shop to buy a box of matches. The assistant handed him a box of the kind that have a riddle or aphorism printed on the back, the purpose of which is to make the smoker smile, or gasp, as he lights his cigarette or pipe. The man, as he turned to leave the shop noticed that, although the brand-name on the box of matches was England's Glory, the riddle on the reverse was in the Welsh language. Offended, and sensitively aware that wedges can have very thin ends indeed, he returned to the counter to demand a replacement by either (a) a box with a riddle in the English language; or (b) a riddle-less box of some other variety.

From time to time you hear or read that people are embarrassed because the streets where they live have Welsh names: they want their Tan-y-bryn or Heol-y-nant replaced by something like Acacia Drive or Fairview Close. The residents of a street in Swansea felt better, perhaps as if a little stain had been washed away, when they changed their street name, Bro Haf, into its English equivalent, Summer Place.

Quite common, I imagine, is the scene I witnessed in a house in south Wales where I was talking with a man and his wife against the familiar background of early evening television. When a news programme in Welsh started, the man scowled and, with his small children looking on, darted across the room saying: 'I won't have that bloody language in my house . . .' and changed channels abruptly.

A complaint that I hear occasionally runs something like this: 'People like you – journalists and broadcasters – talk sentimentally about the Welsh language and give only the minority point of view. Those who support the language, and break the law to underline their demands, get all the attention on television and in the papers. No notice is taken of us, the silent majority, the non-Welsh-speakers.'

Sometimes they add: 'There's going to be big trouble over the language one day because the majority won't be dictated to.'

And occasionally they are more explicit: 'There will be civil war in Wales – and the language will be at the root of it.'

I understand the annoyance that prompts these complaints, and although I have reservations about the concept of a silent majority, I think we have to recognize that there is in Wales a body of people who look on Welsh as a nuisance, a nonsense, an irrelevance, an imposition, even a kind of pollution. They don't want to hear it. They don't want to see it. They don't know much about it, nor do they want to. They believe it is dying and they would not mind much if it were dead. There is genuine irritation felt by many people that because they do not have Welsh they sense they are being looked down on as second-class citizens; that the Welsh-speakers seem to be saying to them that only Welsh-speakers are the 'real Welsh'. The language seems to a considerable number of people in the non-Welsh-speaking majority to be an increasingly irritating piece of grit in the Welsh eye.

Wherever two languages have to exist cheek by jowl there is some potential for friction and even for dangerous tension. However far-fetched such worries may seem, some people do talk in an anxious way about civil war. George Thomas, a former Secretary of State for Wales, once talked of Wales as 'the next Ulster'. People in public life have warned of the dangers of language apartheid, and the coolest of observers have worried about the explosive dangers of linguistic cleavage. There *is* tension today and I believe it is important to ventilate the dislike of Welsh and the suspicions and fears that centre on the language issue and that are a characteristic of life in Wales. There is no escaping the language issue because the strands of it are woven into politics, education, administration, cultural pursuits and social and personal relationships.

It is not possible to know Wales today without understanding something of the way in which the language permeates and how tensions have been created. So we need to look at the background and at the position that Welsh occupies.

The language today is spoken by well over half a million people living in Wales, that is twice the population of Cardiff, the capital. Welsh-speakers are a fifth of the population of Wales and one-hundredth of the population of the United Kingdom. Welsh is an ancient language, perhaps fifteen centuries old, older than English. With some prompting, a well-educated Welshman can read and make sense of manuscripts that were penned by poets in the sixth and seventh centuries. It is a very rich language, too, with a great literature, the oldest living literature in Europe. It is written phonetically and newcomers to the language will find that most words are not difficult to pronounce once they have the hang of Welsh orthography. Although to me Welsh sounds mellifluent, I have to say that some people tell me that to their mind it is gibberish:

'The Welsh and their yuck talk.'

'It's like belching.'

'The wogs begin at Chepstow.'

And so on.

A very large number of people living in the broadly non-Welsh-speaking areas, like Monmouthshire and Glamorgan, say that Welsh to them is as relevant to their daily lives, to their jobs, to the paying of their rates, the buying of postage stamps, the enjoyment of a pint, as Polish or Serbo-Croat or Chinese.

'Welsh?'

'It won't get you anywhere.'

'You don't need it. It's dying.'

'English is a world language.'

'All the Welsh-speakers speak English anyway.'

'What's the use of Welsh?"

'All that money spent on it.'

'All those stupid bilingual forms.'

'And roadsigns.'

'And television programmes.'

'The money could go to spastics.'

'Or hospitals.'

'We spend millions.'

'Just to satisfy the vociferous minority.'

'The hooligans.'

'The middle-class élite.'

'The freemasonry of Welshies.'

'The Taffia!'

'They take all the top jobs.'

'The lifeguard in the swimming pool.'

'Can't swim.'

'How did he get the job?'

'Speaks Welsh.'

'Bilingual education?'

'Learning through a fog of Welsh?'

'Holds the kids back.'

'Rather they learned French.'

'Now we're in the Common Market.'

'The silent majority will hit back.'

'There'll be a backlash.'

'It'll get like Ireland.'

'Welsh never produced a Shakespeare.'

'I don't mind them using it at *eisteddfods*.'

'But when they force it down your throat.'

'I'm all for Welsh.'

'But.'

That 'but' is the biggest 'but' in Wales. It represents the limits that many non-Welsh-speakers have staked out in regard to what they term the 'activities' of Welsh-speakers; and when the Welsh-speakers step over the limit they step on the non-Welsh-speakers' corns of resentment and suspicion; and the shouts are angry ones.

Many visitors to Wales are surprised to find that the Welsh language is not confined to place-names, that it is not patois or pidgin, but that it is widely used as the regular and routine medium of communication in large areas of rural Wales and is the usual speech, too, of many thousands of people who happen to live in the anglicized areas. I know that many people, including visitors I have conducted around Wales, have been fascinated to hear the language in

streets, in pubs, in banks, on the lips of skylarking schoolchildren, in council chambers and in political meetings. In
other words, what surprises visitors is that they come into
contact with something they had not expected to find in the
United Kingdom, another living language.

How is it that, in the last quarter of the twentieth century,
this language is still alive and vigorous, having lived for
many centuries alongside, and been penetrated thoroughly,
by one of the world's mighty languages? Welsh has existed
at the very core of the British Empire, which gave English to
the world, but somehow the Welsh kept a grip on their own
language. It is usual for people to wring their hands over the
numerical decline of Welsh, but it might be better, from time
to time, to celebrate one of the astonishing survival stories
of history.

Troublesome Wales was put under English rule after the
Edwardian conquest of the thirteenth century, and Edward
I's aim was to make Welshmen become, as far as possible,
like Englishmen. But it was not until two and a half centuries later that Wales was incorporated with England in an
Act of Parliament of 1536. Under this legislation, which
sought to tidy up the administration jungle of Wales, English
was instituted as the only language of the administration of
law and public affairs west of Offa's Dyke; Welsh had no
legal validity. From the day the Act became law it became
possible for Welsh fathers to tell their ambitious sons that
they did not need the Welsh language to get on in the world,
advice that has been echoed down the centuries. If young
men wanted to stride the corridors of power in burgeoning
London, then English was the way up – and out. The gentry,
the squires, the merchants and great landowners who had
hitherto been important patrons of Welsh cultural pursuits,
now carried a banner for English and allowed their Welsh
roots to wither. The Welsh language was now in peril, ban-
ished from public life and deserted by its aristocracy who had
given it cash and status. But within thirty years of the Act
which set out to 'extirp' Welsh, a mighty lifeboat was
launched. Queen Elizabeth and her political advisers, fearing the spread of Roman Catholic influence, ordered the publication of a bible in Welsh. Elizabeth was simply being rea-

listic. Whatever her father's legislation was trying to do, Welsh was still the language of most of the people; if they were to hear the true word and not be scalps in the belt of Rome, they must have a Welsh bible. The first translation in 1567, was a masterpiece of obfuscation, but the bible of William Morgan, which appeared twenty-one years later, was a triumph of language. It was revised in 1620 and the importance of it was that it became a cornerstone of education and literature, and Welsh people grew up hearing and using Welsh of high quality. To a considerable extent the bible also standardized the language in Wales and prevented its diffusion into dialects. (A new translation of the New Testament was published in 1975 and a new version of the Old Testament will be published in 1988, exactly four centuries after the publication of the Morgan bible, the book that saved Welsh and ensured the survival of the consciousness of Welsh nationality.)

The nonconformist faith began to spread through Wales in the eighteenth century and became established as a great force in the land in the next century. The language of this movement was the language of the people it served and enfolded: Welsh; and through the chapel schools, the meetings and debates and *eisteddfodau*, as well as services, the ordinary people of Wales became literate people. The basis of their culture was the bible and its good prose, but the people developed wider interests as well and there was a large demand for books.

At the same time the frown of hard-line nonconformity dried some of the laughter in Welsh throats and introduced a sense of guilt into the country people's fun, suffocating much of the dancing and harp playing; though not all. The sensible Welsh saved a lot of it for use in another century.

Only a hundred years ago most of the people of Wales were Welsh-speaking, but the language was being thoroughly undermined. For a long time English people who settled in Wales had been absorbed in the strongly Welsh-speaking communities: the small numbers of newcomers soon developed a broken Welsh to get along with their neighbours, and the children became fluent. But once the trickle of new people became a flow the situation

changed. In south Wales in particular, the immigrants who
came to mine coal and work in the iron industries came in
such large numbers that they did not need to know Welsh; in
any case the native Welsh were rapidly becoming bilingual.
Out in the countryside the occasional English immigrant
family needed a smattering of Welsh as a social and economic necessity, but in the fast-growing towns of the industrial valleys the English language was the common one even
though there was a fair-sized body of Welsh-speakers there.
Some of the mining areas never had a strong Welsh-speaking tradition anyway because, before the coal klondyke, they
had been thinly populated and hardly-known farming
valleys. And Cardiff, the capital-to-be, was essentially a new
city that grew up in the decades at the end of the nineteenth
century and the beginning of the twentieth, a beneficiary of
the rape-economy of the Rhondda and other valleys, and
was never a Welsh-speaking city. In cosmopolitan Cardiff's
bursting youth, the prevalent language was broken English;
the frock-coated coal barons spoke Stock Exchangese.

But there was more threatening Welsh than the sheer
weight of numbers of people who would never need to speak
it. There were strands of social and individual attitudes that,
with economic development, were gradually being spun
together to make a pretty formidable ligature.

Firstly, there was the Welsh sense of inferiority. This had
its seed in English conquest and the stripping away from the
language of its legal and administrative validity in Tudor
times: if you downgrade their language, you downgrade the
people. There was also the steady desertion of the language
by the middle classes, which helped to reduce its status.
There was the growing realization, particularly during the
nineteenth century and the early part of the twentieth, that
fluency in English offered opportunities for advancement
that did not exist for the monoglot Welsh-speaker. There
was the blossoming of the British Empire, the English-
speaking empire. There was the comparatively low level of
national consciousness. There was the report of the commission of 1847 which examined the state of education in
Wales and concluded that Wales was backward – backward
and Welsh-speaking. It fell like a whiplash across Welsh

backs and increased the motivation of the authorities in pressing for the spread of English. There were the Education Acts of 1870 and 1899 which contained no recognition of Welsh and brought a thoroughly English language system of education to the country. There was the notorious Welsh Not, a wooden yoke hung around the necks of children caught speaking Welsh at school. There was the spread of English-language newspapers. There were linguistically mixed marriages in which Welsh usually lost out because children grew up to speak only the common language of their parents. There were the railways which made Wales more accessible to tourists and settlers and aided the spread of English. There was the call of London, the call of America and Australia. There was the First World War: Wales, urged on by Lloyd George, a great recruiting sergeant, gave more than its share of soldiers and lives to help stoke that madness, and many men took on the habit of English in the trenches, as they took on the habit of cigarettes. There was the emptying of the countryside, and of the industrial valleys, too, as Welsh families marched out to new lives, to return only on fleeting visits to grandma. There was the exciting development of radio, then television, mostly in English, so that there was always an English voice at the fireside. There was the continued diminution of Welsh and Welsh history in school syllabuses. By no means all these forces in Welsh life were resented, and many of them were naturally appreciated because most people wanted English and all the culture and vistas it offered. But by the nineteen-sixties the number of Welsh speakers was six hundred and fifty thousand, just over a quarter of the population; and this compared with almost a million only half a century earlier.

Now we come to crucial years. The nineteen-sixties and early seventies represented a watershed in the life of Welsh. These were the years of the great language push when the question of the imperilled language was thrust under the noses of the people of Wales, whether they liked it or not, and placed before the government in Westminster and the administrators in Whitehall. The language question now became a political one.

At the beginning of this period, the early nineteen-sixties, the language was so much in the background in much of Welsh life as to be barely discernible to the majority. For the non-Welsh-speakers living in anglicized areas – and that meant most of the population – Welsh was of little importance and of less interest. For most of them the language question had been settled some time before – and, indeed, for many there was never such a thing as the language question. No, Welsh was an interesting hangover from the old days and the fact that it was fading out was just part of progress. It was quaint that the kids learned the words of the Welsh national anthem at school, and that people still used a few Welsh words like *twp** and *chwarae teg*† in their daily speech; but the majority of people in Wales had shovelled Welsh over the side because it was considered useless – or it had never played any part in their lives anyway because they were not of Welsh stock. For many Welsh-speakers who still lived their lives through Welsh, the decline of the language did not seem a cause for concern because they could not see the overall picture and comprehend the various forms of erosion; they themselves were using the language unselfconsciously as everyone else in their community did. Had they been told that Welsh was dying they would have found it difficult to believe and, anyway, what more could they do when they were using Welsh as naturally as any Englishman used English? Those Welsh-speakers who saw the threats, identified the cause and became alarmed, were relatively small in number and felt helpless. Some of them spoke out at *eisteddfodau*, at political meetings and in the press, worrying about the language and its future; but this was little more than the scratching of a recurring itch on the Welsh skin.

In public and administrative life the Welsh language had no official existence, and this only reinforced the belief of many people, with and without the language, that Welsh was of no use. There was no right of trial in Welsh and hardly any official forms, notices or signs used the language. Secondary schooling was in English almost everywhere in Wales, and the few television programmes in Welsh were

* Daft. † Fair play.

transmitted only when the non-Welsh-speakers were abed. Throughout Wales the footholds of Welsh were cracking and crumbling. And most people were unaware. Those who were aware felt helpless.

But seeds had been sown: seeds of hope for those who cared deeply for the language, seeds of dissension for those who did not care. I have already drawn up a list of the forces that militated against Welsh, the debit side if you like although they were not all unwelcome. But there was also a credit side. Even in the sixteenth century there was a trickling brook of Welsh consciousness, an awareness of the importance of the language; and the source of it was William Salesbury, who wrote and made the first book printed in Welsh. In the eighteenth century this thin stream grew larger as a few writers and academics developed an interest in Welsh culture and history; and from this base grew the consciousness of language and nation that were strong threads in the nineteenth-century story of Wales. Paradoxically, some of the forces that I have noted that worked against the survival of Welsh had aspects or side effects that tended to succour the language. The report of the inquiry into Welsh education and life, in 1847, was a harsh indictment of Wales and Welsh, and only partly true. It was an important influence in stimulating public demand for English education, but it also stung people into thinking more clearly about their country and so it contributed to national awareness. The growth of the mining industry eroded and diluted the language in the long run, but industrial south Wales also acted as a kind of dam, keeping many people within Wales when they were forced to leave, or chose to leave, the rural areas. Ireland had no such dam and so the nineteenth-century exodus from the land was much more socially and culturally crippling there. As late as 1951, more than half the people of the south Wales coalfield were Welsh-speaking. The growth of television, too, has damaged Welsh, but, at the same time, has increased national awareness and consciousness of the language.

Education became a national fetish in Wales and through it the people grabbed their opportunity to get economic, linguistic and social equality with their English neighbours.

Meanwhile, the long struggle to build a national university helped men to clarify their ideas about Wales and was part of the movement for equality, for Welsh emancipation, because it promised to provide poor Wales with the leaders, the middle class of doers, it needed.

The nineteenth century produced a number of Welshmen who felt strongly that Wales was an entity, and their influence is felt today. But some of these nationalists believed that English would have to be the national language, that Wales would always have to be, for its own economic good, part of the English state. They felt strongly enough that Welsh should live, that it should be learned and studied for its own sake, and they appreciated the fact that much of the Welsh public was literate in the old language. But they held that the real work – politics, economics, science and technology – would have to be done in and through English.

On the whole, Welshmen lacked confidence in their language. But there were a number of nationalists in Victorian Wales whose work and words stretch across the years to our own time and play a part in the modern movement to stabilize the Welsh language. Two of the most important were Sir Owen M. Edwards and Emrys ap Iwan. What they did differed but was complementary. Emrys ap Iwan, a Methodist minister, was the spiritual grandfather of the militant Welsh language campaign of the nineteen-sixties and seventies. He made himself unpopular by saying that the survival of the Welsh language was a political issue and he roundly criticized those whose actions and attitudes permitted the erosion of Welsh. O. M. Edwards, who became the chief inspector of schools for Wales, wrote books and magazines which created for his readers a dream of Wales, a country, a community, rich in legend, literature and deeds. His work revealed to many Welshmen the history and culture of their country and told them, perhaps for the first time, about national heroes like Owain Glyndwr. Sir Owen had a lively and readable style of writing and he made the word Wales mean something more than just a geographic term for many of his readers. He was the son of a Merioneth crofter and, as a schoolboy in Llanuwchllyn, had worn the Welsh Not: this attempt to humiliate him had had the effect of making him more determined to keep his language. In 1891 and 1892 he founded Welsh-language magazines for children, and these and the ideals they encompassed, passed to his son, Ifan ab Owen Edwards. In 1922 Sir Ifan started the youth movement Urdd Gobaith Cymru. It was popular from the beginning. Its avowed aim was to serve Christ, fellow-man and Wales – and Wales in this case meant a land of happy, literate Welsh communities, rich in culture, aware of its heritage. The Urdd defends and promotes the language, though lack of Welsh is no bar to membership, and it also provides a lot of fun and interest. It is popular and supported throughout Wales, by Welsh-speakers and non-Welsh-speakers alike, because it is worthy and useful and adopts what many consider is the proper and reasonable approach to winning friends and strength for the language. With forty thousand members it is the largest youth movement in Wales and is a vital agency in the life of Welsh.

Other seeds were planted. The nationalist party, *Plaid Cymru,* was founded in 1925, and in its infancy was a small band of writers and teachers seeking to conserve the language. The Welsh schools movement, which set out to provide Welsh-medium education in anglicized areas, started in 1939. The first bilingual comprehensive school opened in Wales in 1956.

But no one could doubt that Welsh was like a sandcastle before a relentless tide. The erosion of it, by the nineteen-sixties, was so rapid that it appeared possible that it would be effectively lost, that is unable to regenerate and sustain itself, by the beginning of the twenty-first century.

It was against this immediate background, and the historical background, that Saunders Lewis, the astringent and enigmatic old writer and critic, one of the founders of *Plaid Cymru* and an influential figure in nationalist thinking, went to the microphone in February 1962 to deliver the BBC Wales annual lecture. It was a powerful exposition of the decline of the language and a sombre warning of its desperate position. He called for action, for revolution, to save the language. 'Go to it,' he said. For its far-reaching consequences the Saunders Lewis broadcast was the most significant in the history of broadcasting in Wales.

Within a year, in response to this appeal, there was formed *Cymdeithas yr Iaith Gymraeg*, the Welsh Language Society, which, in the next dozen years, earned for itself a mixture of respect and hatred, admiration and contempt. The organization and its effect were remarkable. Most of the members of the society were university students. They may be seen, with some justification, as part of the general movement of student discontent and protest which erupted in many parts of the world during that decade. But *Cymdeithas yr Iaith* did not ride any old band-wagon of protest that happened along. Its members became suffused with anger at the way their language had deteriorated, had been allowed to deteriorate. They looked around with young eyes and saw that the sentries had been asleep. They decided to ring the bells. Like other groups, like Negroes and Red Indians for example, they saw that they would have to campaign for civil rights; only, in their case, civil rights for their native language which, at that time, had no official existence. Unlike many inchoate student groups, they saw for themselves a clear task: to sting, hard and often.

They stung in several ways: they stung Welsh-speakers themselves, drew their attention to the condition of the language, implied that they were an apathetic lot who were letting their heritage slip from their grasp, and asked them what they were going to do about it. They stung non-Welsh-speakers, made many of them aware that a possession that belonged to all of Wales was being lost. They stung local authorities, the big institutions and the government. The techniques of protest varied. There were some mistakes and foolishness, and some of the protest involved breaking the law. But most of the demonstrations were effective in that they continued the process of stinging and of asking questions that needed answering, and they got publicity. The sit-down protest, in roads and television studios, the marches, rallies and demonstrations in court rooms became familiar on television and in the newspapers. The Welsh Language Society had a fairly well-developed sense of publicity.

The effects of all this 'stinging' were varied. Many young Welsh-speakers were thrilled by the language fighters' exploits and their brushes with the law, and hurried to join.

Many people of an older generation were moved by what they saw and identified readily with the struggle for recognition. Overtly, or otherwise, they supported what the demonstrators were doing. But numbers of Welsh-speakers were appalled. They felt embarrassed, did not want their own children to become part of the trouble, and thought the demonstrators were forfeiting goodwill for the language in exchange for a few buff forms printed in Welsh. In anglicized Wales there was a strong feeling against the young protesters although, here also, there was sympathy and a jolting into awareness. The language society was loathed, perhaps most of all, for its colourfully expressed opposition to the investiture of the Prince of Wales at Caernarfon on the grounds that it was a calculated insult to stage an expensive State ceremony which only emphasized Welsh subjection to English domination.

The language society started life by asking for bilingual official forms, like summonses and applications and car tax discs. There was a quiet period from 1963–5 while a committee under the chairmanship of Sir David Hughes-Parry met to consider the legal status of Welsh. The committee recommended the principle of equal validity for Welsh and English, meaning that any document in Welsh would be as valid in Wales as if it had been written in English, and this concept was incorporated into the Welsh Language Act of 1967. It was a step forward, but not by any means enough for the young men and women of the language society who felt an urgent need to do something for Welsh, to make real achievements, not paper ones. There were three main campaigns: a demand for bilingual forms, now being met increasingly by the authorities and organizations like the Post Office since the language act came into force; a demand for bilingual roadsigns; a demand for a better broadcasting service for Wales, including a Welsh-language channel. All the campaigns were carried on simultaneously, although there were times when there was greater emphasis on a particular one. But at no time were the aims of the young campaigners totally out of touch with other sections of society. To a greater or lesser degree they represented the feelings of a considerable portion of the Welsh public. There were many who professed to agree with their aims, if not their methods.

No one imagined that bilingual forms and roadsigns, by themselves, would save the Welsh language. They would help to improve the common vocabulary. But that was not the whole point. The point was to awaken people, to demonstrate a new determination and confidence and a will to survive. The aim of *Cymdeithas yr Iaith* was to secure the right, and the official wherewithal, to live their lives as far as possible through their language. They wanted to be able to do almost anything in Welsh in their dealings with the administration and the law that could be done in English. That would give the language an essential dignity and recognition. The administration eventually conceded the justice of this claim. Dignity and recognition do not, by themselves, save a language, either, but official recognition and support carry weight and help to influence public attitudes.

The authorities dug in their heels, however, on the matter of bilingual roadsigns, and the activists began a campaign of daubing and uprooting signs which did not carry the Welsh name of a town. They argued that Welsh could not have dignity while it was ignored on the most public of signs. Many of those responsible for daubing gave themselves up to the police, and this opened the way to renewed campaigning for the right of trial in Welsh, a right that, in practice, the law could only meet with great difficulty. Meanwhile, people were refusing to buy television licences to mark their dissatisfaction with the quantity of Welsh on radio and television; and to reinforce the demand for a Welsh channel. These were not only young people: these were mature people, some of them well known.

From 1969 to 1972 there were demonstrations, struggles with police, arrests, chanting and singing. Language campaigners disrupted the courts and were fined and imprisoned. Interpreters were brought in, but they lacked training and knowledge of legal terms and trials were reduced almost to farce. In order that the courts could maintain dignity, and indeed could keep to the law, the Lord Chancellor ordered an inquiry into the question of Welsh in the courts.

The campaigners received a lot of publicity. Angry letters poured into newspapers and to the broadcasters' offices to express outrage at what was going on. Fresh fuel was added when some magistrates clubbed together to pay the fine of the language society's leader, Dafydd Iwan, and procured his release from prison. The Lord Chancellor, the Master of the Rolls and the Attorney-General warned the magistracy that any JP who showed bias would be removed from the bench. There was a fresh row when five magistrates at Bala gave absolute discharges to a minister and four teachers who had refused to buy television licences. Many people regarded this affair as a scandal and complained that old-age pensioners were being fined ten pounds for having no licence, while language campaigners were being discharged. But the Bala case was a rare occurrence and most benches applied the same penalties to the 'conscientious objectors' as to everyone else. Nevertheless, for a considerable number of magistrates, the stint on the local bench brought the prospect of an agonizing struggle with conscience. In Swansea a magistrate disagreed with her colleagues in a particular case and paid a language offender's fine. She had to resign. Some JPs were uncomfortable because they found themselves dealing, not with the usual run of delinquents, inadequates and local scallywags, but with pillars of local education and chapel, with academics and serious students. A magistrate said to me: 'I dread the day that one of these conscientious language campaigners appears before me. The way that my sympathies run, I know I would be in the dock with him if I were younger.'

For people involved in the Welsh cause these were heady days. Moving among them one could sense an electric atmosphere and catch the excitement of young people with a sense of mission. *I'r gad!* said their posters and stickers: To battle!

For many older Welsh speakers there was also a sense of excitement, a feeling of revival. Critics accused them of egging the young people on to break the law, of getting a vicarious pleasure out of a struggle that they themselves should have fought a generation before.

For many others there was deep concern that the language

had become a battleground. They did not like it. And the vehemence with which some of them criticized the campaigners was more furious than that of most non-Welsh-speakers who attacked the language society.

There were many people who thought that the situation was decidedly ugly. They felt threatened and wondered, if Welsh-speakers got their way, whether Welsh was to be almost a condition of living in Wales. Others pointed to their own language-less Welshness – their close valley communities, their socialism, their internationalist traditions – and asked what place could Welsh have in their lives. By all means speak it, they said, learn it, teach it to your children, have your own television channel – but don't force it down our throats or our children's throats.

George Thomas, Secretary of State for Wales from 1968 to 1970, reacted strongly. Never far from controversy during his long Parliamentary career, he flailed frequently at nationalism. He was a product of the Rhondda, and proud of his background. He was brought up in a Rhondda eroded by want in which, he says, he saw people rotting without hope. The Methodist chapel and the Labour party were his beacons and for him, and many others, the party represented the road to a better life for valleys people. He could only be scathing to any threat to the party, and the eruption of nationalism in the nineteen-sixties worried him. 'Any threat to Labour and I was after it like a shot,' he said to me.

He was unable to be objective and unemotional about nationalism, and found it difficult to come to terms with the forces for change in Wales, and in his own party. To him the Welsh language struggle was part of the nationalist threat, and he was the first public figure in Wales to use the emotive analogy of 'Wales the next Ulster'. He even offered himself as a rallying-point for any English-only Welshmen who wanted to form a group to counter the Welsh Language Society. 'There are signs we are hellbent for what Ulster got,' he said. 'It may be practical politics to talk of a partition in Wales as there is in Ulster.'

George Thomas admits that he was sensitive about Welsh, but says that he did not hate the language. His linguistic background was typical of that of many valleys people. His father and stepfather were Welsh-speaking and his grandmother was unable to speak a word of English and young George had to speak to her in Welsh. So he had childhood Welsh and, he says, he learned some more when he moved to the Welsh Office. But – and this may be significant – 'people laughed at my mistakes. That really got under my skin and I think it was a cause of my unhappy relationship with the Welsh Language Society. I was a bit rough on the Welsh language people, especially in the beginning, but I had genuine fears of a divided Wales, and I gave way to my weakness for exaggeration.'

There is no doubt, though, that many people felt Mr Thomas was saying the right thing, standing up for the silent majority which watched the demonstrations and disruption with increasing concern. His critics called him the Enoch Powell, or the Alf Garnett, of the language issue; but others said he performed a service in voicing the anger of South Wales Man and his feeling of being threatened. In retrospect, it seems that Mr Thomas was miscast at the Welsh Office in that sensitive period. He acted as if he were appointed to be the hammer of the nats; but that was a time that needed a cooler man in the Welsh Office, a conciliator, a bridge builder, a statesman. After all, it did have the makings of a serious situation. In a reflective moment Mr Thomas commented on Harold Wilson's decision to give the Welsh Office to John Morris in 1974, while Mr Thomas became deputy Speaker of the Commons. 'I think history will show that it was right for John Morris to be secretary of state,' he said.

Peter Thomas, the Conservative secretary of state from 1970 to 1974, set up a committee to investigate the question of bilingual roadsigns and the campaign for them was effectively brought to an end. Meanwhile, on the orders of the Lord Chancellor, work was going on to equip certain crown courts with a system of simultaneous translation, and the first case where this system was used was heard in Cardiff in 1973. A panel of interpreters was established, receiving a retainer of two hundred pounds a year plus a fee for each of their sessions in the sound-proof booth in the court room.

There were plans for similarly equipped courts at Carmarthen and Mold.

In the difficult field of broadcasting, too, there were important steps being taken to bring peace to Wales, and a better deal for the Welsh language. Every day in Wales the sight of the titles of Welsh language programmes rolling up on the screens sent thousands of viewers lunging like scrum-halves to change channels, or out to the television dealers to get an aerial that would pick up the transmissions from English masts and cut out Welsh, and Wales itself, from their screens. Welsh-speakers, on the other hand, were looking at their television rations and sending off protests which were variations on a theme made famous by Oliver Twist. At the same time, the mountains compounded the linguistic difficulties of the broadcasters by making reception in many areas poor, maddening, or non-existent. In this situation, the report of the Crawford committee, in 1974, recommending that there should be a Welsh language television service on the fourth channel, and that improvement of reception should be a priority, was welcomed by almost everyone in Wales. The language campaigners, and many other people, felt there was now an opportunity to provide a good television service for Wales and the Welsh language; and those who were irritated by Welsh on their screens saw the prospect of saying good-bye to it, if not good riddance.

In the meantime the committee on bilingual roadsigns had recommended that there should indeed be a transition to bilingual signs, and with Welsh on top. There was a need to play for more time, so the government put the matter in the hands of the Road Research Laboratory which reported that signs could be marginally safer with English on top, but the report was essentially inconclusive and the published statistics showed that it did not matter much either way. The matter was further investigated by the laboratory, with much the same result, but John Morris felt it was good enough to enable him to authorize bilingual signs, with English on top.

At the end of 1973 Peter Thomas, responding to the mood of concern about the language, set up the Council for the Welsh Language. Its brief was to work for the welfare of

Welsh, to promote it and defend it, while trying to create an atmosphere of greater understanding and tolerance between Welsh-speaker and non-Welsh-speaker.

So, by the end of 1973, the period of demonstrations, court scenes and jailings, was largely over. The fairly familiar faces of language campaigners had faded from the television screens. The campaign had succeeded in putting the Welsh question firmly before the public and had stimulated action. The Welsh Language Society was a catalyst and was largely unpopular for the way it went about its business. But direct action was at the heart of its philosophy, and direct action had worked. There had been civil disobedience and lawbreaking, but because most people in the movement accepted the creed of non-violence there was little violence of a physical kind. There had been some cuts and bruises sustained by demonstrators and police during the demonstrations where emotions were on the boil, but no one was killed or seriously injured. The language society had been led and united in the crucial years by Dafydd Iwan, an architect, a folk singer, a man of courage and integrity who, throughout, retained his humour, his cool, and his utter determination.

It was inevitable that the language campaign should alienate some people and exacerbate tensions. Anyone who acts with the intention of doing good seems to do some bad as well. Gwynfor Evans, president of *Plaid Cymru*, said wryly that the activities of the campaigners had cost him his Parliamentary seat in Carmarthen in 1970. But he naturally approved of the efforts made by the campaigners, and, indeed, his daughter Meinir was a leading demonstrator.

The Welsh Language Society was small – its maximum membership was four thousand – young, noisy, idealistic, with all the virtues and faults of any group fired with a sense of mission. It banged a great drum for Welsh, and, however distasteful its methods were to the majority of the people in Wales, however much it got under their skins, it performed an important service. Moreover, such a movement was inevitable.

But it should be remembered that the language society is only one part, the spiky part, of the Welsh language movement. It could never have worked in a vacuum and it was effective in its most publicized campaigns because it was part of a larger movement which had, and has, a similar aim: the survival of Welsh. The language movement is many-faceted and almost entirely respectable and some parts of it have government support and royal patronage. There is the national *eisteddfod,* the whole *eisteddfod* movements for nursery schools, for youth, for women, for adult learners, and many others.

With the ending of the direct action campaigning, the Welsh Language Society found itself at a cross-roads, even a loose end. What was it to do, now that there was a new climate for Welsh? The society began to change and to look at past achievements and wonder about the future. Dafydd Iwan relinquished the chairmanship, although remaining an important figure in the movement and editor of its magazine, and stood as a *Plaid Cymru* Parliamentary candidate in Anglesey in 1974. Another leading campaigner said: 'Some of us have been active in the language campaign for more than ten years. We are in our thirties now and, while we saw things as black and white when we were in our twenties, we now see the shades of grey.' Not only that, the police and the Director of Public Prosecutions office had shown themelves perfectly willing to use the dubious technique of the conspiracy charge in an effort to crush the language campaign, and young men with families faced the prospect of long prison sentences.

With the steam gone from direct action campaigning, some groups of young people felt deflated and discontented and yearned for the heroic days of demonstrations. There were some who said the language society was too soft and middle-of-the-road, who said that the authorities only responded to violence. Ffred Ffransis, secretary of *Cymdeithas yr Iaith*, who had been to prison several times during the campaign, said to me: 'There are people outside the society who think we don't act strongly enough – and they do not approve of our belief that we should take responsibility for our actions: own up to the police. Obviously this is a dangerous situation, and I think we are the only people who can stop violence by channelling anger into nonviolent action. What we have to do is find an effective way of acting on questions like second homes and we recognize that we cannot operate in a vacuum. We have to gain more support from the people. We cannot force change in favour of the language just by working through the authorities. The will for change has to come from the Welsh people. One of our important tasks now is to win the confidence of people, show our faces and talk to them. We need to demonstrate to them that the battle for the language has a direct relevance to their lives, that the threats to their jobs and communities are allied to the threats which erode the language. People have been frightened or outraged by our direct action in the past, and poor public relations has been one of our weaknesses. Now we want people to understand and I now believe that direct action without preparing the ground in this way is unthinkable. But there will have to be direct action. People have listened to us only because we are a society of activists. We are told that more agitation will only alienate people and damage the goodwill that exists for the language. But I liken the language to a man who is drowning while crowds look on. They all bear him goodwill – but they do not dive in to save him.'

An important effect of the language campaign was that it made many people more keenly aware that creation of the conditions for language survival was going to be no easy task. Demonstrations had a certain value in certain circumstances, official support and recognition were a vital prerequisite, but when the shouting died there was much work to do at the places where the language was being eroded.

It was no longer enough to go out on the streets of Wales and shout: '1536!' and rage against the injuries done by the Welsh Not.

Offshoots of the language movement, trying to build new dykes, are the small housing groups set up to fight rearguard actions in the Welsh countryside against the steady growth of second-home ownership. The summer houses, the *tai haf*, are a many-sided issue. The buying-up by outsiders of fairly remote cottages and houses in forests, or on mountain-sides and cliffs, does little harm and saves many buildings from

becoming derelict. The activity also creates work and trade
for local craftsmen and shops. But trouble, real erosion,
starts when outsiders buy up houses in village centres. They
can afford to outbid local people, often deprive young
couples of the opportunity of getting a home and contribute
to the break-up of communities. The housing groups (there
are only a handful at present) buy houses, renovate them
with the aid of local paid craftsmen or volunteers, and let
them to local families who would not otherwise be able to
afford a home and might leave the district. The housing
groups' struggle to keep cottages in Welsh hands is, of
course, grossly unequal. The groups do not have the re-
sources to compete with the increasing numbers of English
people looking for country retreats. 'But doing something,
however small, is better than wringing our hands,' Mr Maldwyn Lewis, one of the founders of *Cymdeithas Tai Gwynedd*, the north Wales group, said. Another group is *Adfer* –
the word means restoration – whose chairman is Emyr
Llywelyn. He was once a chairman of the Welsh Language
Society and says that *Adfer's* work is more relevant to
working-class people in the country than the demonstrations of the language campaigners.

One of the most remarkable movements for community
renewal in rural Wales is going on in Llanaelhaearn, a small
one-school, one-pub village which lies beneath Yr Eifl
mountain in the Lleyn peninsula. A few years ago this village was dying. Depopulation, a lack of work and second-
home ownership on an increasing scale was knocking the
stuffing out of the village. It seemed certain to deteriorate,
like many other villages, into a husk. It was the new village
doctor who diagnosed Llanaelhaearn's sickness and prescribed a form of treatment. Carl Clowes, son of a Welsh
mother and an English father, and brought up in Manchester, was doing cancer research in Manchester when he
saw an advertisement for a single-handed rural dispensing
practice at Llanaelhaearn. It was exactly what he wanted, a
practice where doctor and patients could form a real bond.
He had some Welsh and he looked forward to giving his
children a Welsh country upbringing. 'But even as we
settled in, the crisis in rural Wales was brought home viv-

idly. The local quarry closed, the bus service to a nearby village was stopped, two shops closed and the council was about to close the village school. If we had not acted then the community would have fallen apart. Although some people thought it pointless to take on bureaucracy, we won our battle for the school and this gave us confidence. We were told that nobody would want to be headmaster of a small school like ours, but we insisted on the post being advertised and there were thirty-six applicants. When we saved the school it had twenty-seven pupils. Soon it had forty-two.'

Encouraged by that success the people formed a village society to campaign for improvements, and the next step was to form a limited company, Antur Aelhaearn (*antur* means venture and Aelhaearn was the sixth-century saint from which the village takes its name). Only the two hundred and sixty people on the electoral roll were entitled to buy the one pound voting shares, and they could buy only one share each; but anybody could buy loan stock at nine per cent. Turning the village into a limited company was an act of faith and a focus for the people's hopes.

'Our aim is to help ourselves,' Dr Clowes said, 'to provide work for young people, to retain our community and our Welshness. We must create jobs, and jobs for men especially; there will always be people who want to leave the countryside to make their lives elsewhere, but we have a responsibility to provide a choice, the opportunities for those who want to live and work close to their roots.'

The village paid for a factory and rented it to a fancy goods firm. That was a start. A London company helped with the setting up of a knitting workshop and trained the supervisor. A potter moved to the village, began to learn Welsh and took on an apprentice, a local boy. Within a year of the founding of the company two former holiday homes had been bought back for occupation by local people and Dr Clowes said he hoped that eventually all of them would be back in the possession of villagers. 'Holiday homes make no contribution to our village life.' He hopes that the government will find a way of helping villages like Llanaelhaearn which show that they are willing to help themselves. Big factories, he says, are not always the answer in rural areas; jobs and homes have to be restored in twos and threes, fitting in with the character of small communities. The fundamental part of Dr Clowes's motivation is the Welsh language. His Irish wife has learned it and it is now the language of his home and of the children, Dafydd, Rhiannon and Angharad. 'Yes, the language is the catalyst. I want Llanaelhaearn to be a thriving and Welsh-speaking community. Because its problems are in the Welsh context, I and the others have an extra drive to do something.' In a way the village burns a beacon in rural Wales and other communities wonder if it holds the key to their own futures. The decline of villages, with young people drifting away, has been breaking up a way of life and a well-tried set of values. The emptying of the hills causes not only a drop in morale among those who stay; it creates frustration and anger. While many young people still leave the country, along the well-beaten path to England, either from choice or no-choice, there is a growing number whose sense of commitment to Wales keeps them in the country. They recognize the need to act as well as talk, to back up their idealism with a healthy sense of commercialism and economics.

While some communities and individuals work to keep the language in its strongholds, many people are working hard to acquire it. The study of Welsh is the most popular evening class subject in anglicized south and north-east Wales, even in Monmouthshire. The number of adult learners, although it runs into many thousands, is unlikely to make an appreciable difference to the overall number of Welsh-speakers, but the classes are evidence of the interest there is in the language. The motivation of learners varies. Some young parents go to classes because they have sent their children to Welsh-medium schools – schools where Welsh is the medium of instruction – and they want to be able to share in their education; they sent their children to Welsh-medium schools because they felt it was important for them to enjoy both the cultures of Wales. Others feel a sense of loss or deprivation because they are without Welsh. A pillar of the Welsh Establishment said to me that he did not transmit Welsh to his son because he thought the language was dying but one day the boy beat his father on the chest, crying: 'Why didn't you give me my language?' And then spent years learning it. There is a view that the interest in learning Welsh is only a passing phase of romance, but I suspect that if Welsh could be grafted into mind and memory through some science-fiction subliminal technique, at least half the non-Welsh-speaking public would undergo the treatment. Greater awareness of heritage, the standardization of the language and better teaching methods have contributed to the popularity of Welsh lessons. The dull grammars of old have been replaced by tape-courses, cassettes for stereo-Welsh in the car, film strips and well-produced books with plenty of modern idiom. Where the old grammars had staid and unlikely phrases such as 'The teacher is in the field,' or 'The archdruid is under the umbrella,' the new Welsh manuals contain sentences like 'She has hellish big breasts', and 'Turn the TV off and come to the pub.'

As with any language, learners find a gulf between wish and fulfilment. Enthusiasm wanes if motivation is not strong enough, and the recognition of this led to the founding of the Institute of Wales, an organization of Welsh-learners. Apart from teaching people in small units it operates, in a sense, like Alcoholics Anonymous, in that people who feel their resolve weakening can make contact with fellow-learners and have their flagging interest revived.

The nearest that some learners get to the ideal of a Welsh injection is the *ulpan* course. *Ulpan* is a Hebrew word and the technique of the intensive language course was developed in Israel as a matter of urgency soon after that state was founded, and large numbers of people, speaking many languages, started to emigrate there and there was a need for a common tongue. In Wales the first *ulpan* course started in Cardiff in 1973 with ten people paying five pounds each for a one-hundred-hour course, two hours a night, five nights a week engrossed in conversation with four volunteer teachers. The encouraging outcome of that pilot run led to the founding of courses all over Wales, run by local authorities, the University of Wales and voluntary groups. Soon there were waiting lists for courses. While, for most learners, the

motivation is cultural, social or academic, some people have
an economic motive. To meet this requirement the University of Wales started a three-month *ulpan* course in 1975, in
which students are immersed in Welsh for three hours every
morning. The cost was seventy pounds and in many cases it
was met by employers who were anxious to have more
Welsh-speaking staff. For the students the courses sometimes improved their chances of promotion. The Midland
Bank was one of the first employers to send men on the
intensive *ulpan* because there was a shortage of Welsh-
speaking staff in Welsh-speaking areas, and customers
wanted to do business through Welsh. Christopher Rees,
language research officer at the University of Wales, said
that results were surprisingly good. 'Naturally, people learn
at different rates and I would say that four out of ten
become competent after a hundred hours. That is, they
can dispense with English and hold their own socially
with Welsh-speakers. There is a shortage of certain kinds
of skilled people in Welsh-speaking areas and employers
recognize that if they are to give the sort of service customers want, more of their employees will need Welsh.'

It was not just the increasing army of learners that emphasized the strength of the language revival. There was evidence enough that more parents wanted their children to
have education through the medium of Welsh, from nursery,
through primary school to secondary school. The nursery
schools movement grew quickly in the nineteen-seventies
and it was here that those anxious about the decline of
Welsh saw the best hope for the future. The first bilingual
comprehensive school was opened at Rhyl in 1956, the
second at Mold in 1961, the third at Rhydfelen, Pontypridd,
in 1962, with others following at Wrexham, Ystalyfera in
the Swansea valley, at Aberystwyth and at Llanharry in
Glamorgan. Rhydfelen is a particularly interesting school
because, being in the heart of anglicized south Wales, only a
fifth of the one thousand pupils come from Welsh-speaking
homes. For many parents it used to be an act of faith, and
for some an act of courage, to send their children to a school
like Rhydfelen. But today it is no longer a leap in the dark:
the school is no longer a daring experiment. The demand for

the kind of education it provides is swelling. Rhydfelen started with eighty pupils and when its population topped the thousand another school had to be built to cope with the demand.

The bilingual comprehensives teach the arts, including foreign languages, through the medium of Welsh, and mathematics and the sciences, and English, through the medium of English. The teachers have had to be, to some extent, pioneers and because of the shortage of certain Welsh text books they have had to write their own and also create other material. When the schools started there were sceptics who feared that bilingual education might be incomplete and harmful. But these fears have proved groundless and have been answered by higher-than-average academic results, manifestly happy school populations and satisfied parents. Although many English-only parents send their children to these schools, it was the Welsh-speakers, in the early days, who had to be convinced that Welsh-medium education would not put their children behind. Once they became satisfied about the schools' academic standards the schools began to grow. The motives of non-Welsh-speaking parents whose children have Welsh-medium education are varied but there is a fairly common theme. A mother said to me: 'My parents were Welsh-speaking but did not pass the language to me because they believed it was useless and the emphasis at that time was on getting on in the world, getting on at all costs. They thought Welsh would get in my way and would be a baggage I could do without. They deliberately cut me off from the language that was part of our tradition and they did it for what they thought were the best reasons. They gave no thought of the cultural loss and I cannot blame them because the climate was very different then. But I do feel the loss deeply, partly because so many of my relatives have kept their Welsh and because there is so much that is enjoyable going on in Welsh. I feel that people like me represent a missing link and I was determined that my children should have the pleasure of their native language, that I should do my bit to reconnect the chain. Apart from anything else they have benefited educationally. I am not one of these language zealots and I am not saying that a

Welsh education is right for everyone. But the great interest that many people show in the language, quite ordinary people without any axe to grind, is an indication to me that our society has a healthy concern for its roots.'

There is a special atmosphere in schools like Rhydfelen. It is obvious that parental involvement is strong and that the staff are dedicated. A former headmaster at Rhydfelen, Gwilym Humphries, said: 'Of course, we are here to help and enhance the Welsh language – but we are here primarily to educate. This is a bilingual school and there is no compulsion to speak Welsh. Pupils may talk in whatever language they wish. We aim to be a community where people are as free as possible. I think that one of the benefits of bilingual education is that it generates self-confidence. I recall that when I left school I felt uncertain and even second-rate in the presence of English-speakers because of my native language. But students at Rhydfelen never feel inferior. They are at home in any situation. In a school with strong parental support and a full social life, we give them self-confidence and so help to restore self-respect to Welsh people.'

The new waves of interest in Welsh, from the nineteen-sixties onward, offered the paradox of a language shrinking numerically, yet a language more vigorous than it had ever been. It had traditionally been a language of the hearth, of the market place, the chapel, the *eisteddfod*, of poetry, and of a large number of worthy books. Now it lives on television, on radio, in pop music and magazines and a much broader range of books. And in the law courts and administration, too. But the more the language was modernized, was made more relevant and spread, the larger that some of the gaps seemed to be. And the new mood was to ensure that whatever was being done in English should at least be attempted in Welsh.

One of the interesting aspects of life in Wales now is the devotion with which some people are sticking their thumbs in Offa's Dyke, not so much to keep English out as to keep Welshness in; and the Welsh language movement aims to develop the language and give it fresh expression, as well as shore it up. And one of the gaps in Welsh expression was the lack of native cinema. Today, however, a small group of people is making up for lost time and a Welsh Film Board has been set up to co-ordinate the efforts and finance films. The leading film-maker is Will Aaron, formerly a director with the BBC's *24 Hours* and *Midweek*, who returned to Wales with a strong feeling that a Welsh cinema should be established. He draws on his considerable television experience to make films quickly and at relatively small cost, using natural locations and never expensive sets. 'I get more satisfaction from making films in Welsh, a culture I know and care about, and I get more response to them from Welsh audiences than I would from equivalent films in English.'

The first Welsh film was made during the nineteen-thirties by Sir Ifan ab Owen Edwards, founder of the Welsh youth movement. He made a documentary about quarrymen in north Wales and cut a soundtrack on large discs. With a mobile generator powering a projector, the film toured the country, playing to large audiences in village halls. It was the first 'talkie' seen in many parts of Wales ... and an elderly woman, seeing someone speak Welsh on the screen, fainted away. A few Welsh films were made in 1947, but no more were produced until Welsh-language television started in the sixties. To Welsh people the cinema has always meant Hollywood and Pinewood – but that is beginning to change now. One of the most difficult problems is distribution. 'We show films at *eisteddfodau*,' Will Aaron said, 'but because many cinemas in Wales have closed we shall have to put on shows in village halls and small theatres, reviving the travelling cinema that Sir Ifan pioneered in the thirties.'

In broadcast entertainment there are also gaps to be filled; but there are many who are anxious about the demands that a fourth television channel carrying a fuller Welsh language service will make on performing and writing talent. Ryan Davies, the comedian and character actor who made an enormous contribution to the development of television humour and light entertainment in Wales and in Welsh, said: 'If something is in Welsh on television it has to be first class because no one is going to put up with rubbish out of loyalty if he can switch over and get something better in English.'

Ryan Davies cared deeply about Welsh. He was the only comedian in Britain who worked in two languages and he was the only performer in Welsh language comedy who achieved the rank of star. Although more comic actors are developing now, there is a sense in which Ryan Davies was the backbone of television comedy in Welsh and he felt a sense of responsibility for that reason. 'Although I'm like anyone else in entertainment – I have my ego and I want national recognition in Britain – I want to keep one foot in Wales. It is my home and I want to contribute to the development of Welsh entertainment. I want to hang on to my identity, too. I would hate to hear people mutter that Ryan Davies had gone English and deserted his own people.'

In England, comedians traditionally got their grounding in music-hall and variety; now they progress through cabaret, clubs, radio and television. But there was never any Welsh-language music-hall and radio was limited and television is very young. Welsh comedy is rooted in the intimate Saturday night gatherings called *noson lawen* – merry evenings – and also in the *eisteddfod* and humorous verses and witty word battles. Ryan Davies was entirely a product of this background and acquired self-confidence and a taste for entertaining at *eisteddfodau*, the 'Opportunity Knocks' of Wales. 'Working in two languages is bound to be fulfilling for a comedian,' Ryan Davies said, 'though marginally I prefer working in Welsh on television because it is a more intimate experience for me to work in my first language, and I feel more my real self.'

Although broadcasting will, increasingly, be a prime source of energy of Welsh, there is also a strong supporting role played by publishing. Literature in Wales, in Welsh and in English, has a new drive and the standards of poetry and prose improve each year. Publishing in Welsh, like publishing anywhere, is beset by problems of accelerating costs, and few books in Welsh are published without the support of a grant. Many publishers have for a long time been unbusinesslike and have been content with only average standards of production. But during the past few years a number of publishing houses have made themselves much more professional and commercial and the best productions compare with anything published in London. The Welsh Books Council, with its advice on design, editing and marketing, and the Welsh Arts Council, have done much to improve standards. There is today a greater variety of books published in Welsh and it is no longer true that a Welsh book is always a serious book. The Books Council, indeed, wants to see more light novels and books of pure entertainment written in the old language. And the need for more books for children, although there has been great improvement in this field, is a pressing one. Publishers in Welsh have to reconcile themselves to the fact that their market is relatively small and that the tradition of cheap books in Welsh dies hard: many readers find it difficult to appreciate that the day of the ten-and-sixpenny hard cover has gone. There are a number of good periodicals for children and adults, and some mediocre ones, too. They are all grappling with economic difficulties. The children's magazines seem to me to be a critical element in language survival, not only for their educational value, but because they provide an essential humour, nonsense and escapism which children should be able to get from Welsh comics as well as English ones.

There are six weekly newspapers and a handful of newssheets published in Welsh, selling about forty thousand copies a week. The circulation of the leading newspaper, *Y Cymro*,* is about eight thousand, and of *Barn*,† the leading journal of opinion and review, about three thousand. Considering the noises made from time to time by people anxious that Welsh should live a full life, these circulations seem low. Of course, there is no reason why people should buy Welsh publications that do not interest them. But some of the armchair critics might do better to take the periodicals and see what they can do about writing to them, and writing for them, with the aim of building a more flourishing, a more informing, Welsh press.

Something missing from the press in Wales is the kind of cross-reporting which would help to create greater understanding between Welsh-speakers and non-Welsh-speakers and would help to strengthen links between the regions and communities of Wales. BBC Wales, for example, takes

* *The Welshman.*   † *Opinion.*

What The Papers Say from London, but does not add a selection from the *Western Mail*, the *Daily Post* and, where appropriate, from *Y Cymro*. Non-Welsh-speaking listeners should surely be told what the Welsh-language press is saying on certain issues. Similarly, the *Western Mail* and the *Daily Post* might review the Welsh press on a regular basis. Both the broadcasters and the newspapers are missing an opportunity to inform better.

All the Welsh papers exist, not only to serve their public, but also the language in which they are printed. None could exist on its own. Some of the papers find it increasingly difficult to get enough advertising and many advertisements, anyway, are in English. Apart from their economic difficulties the Welsh papers have to think hard about their role and content because of the competition of radio, tele-vision and English-language papers. *Y Cymro* and *Y Faner** have the problem of trying to be national papers, eschewing purely local news, and to some extent are maga-zines.

In the golden age of Welsh language journalism, during the second half of the nineteenth century, papers flourished and many people received their news through Welsh; and not just local news, but national and also international news. *Y Faner* had a London correspondent who supplied a definite Welshman's view of Parliamentary and home affairs. Thomas Gee, who founded *Y Faner* in 1947, made his journal a great newspaper; it was a campaigning paper and fought for the country people, the quarrymen and the farmers, and was also an entertaining paper, one of the ear-liest 'popular' newspapers in Britain. Today the paper has to struggle to keep going. It is as much a tradition as a news-paper and lives because its supporters give money to a sur-vival fund and because its printers believe in it. And there is also the dedicated work of its editor, Gwilym R. Jones, and the assistant editor, Mathonwy Hughes, both in their sev-enties. Critics of the paper yearn for the sort of writing that made the paper famous, but the editor says it retains con-siderable influence – 'Its job is to help give the Welsh people backbone.' Gwilym R. Jones recalls that he once worked

* The popular name for *Baner ac Amserau Cymru*.

with people who had worked with Thomas Gee, and remembers a time when, in his father's shop in north Wales, there was always a large pile of copies of *Y Faner*, but only two copies of the *Liverpool Daily Post* because only two people in the village could read English. Over the years he saw the *Post* pile grow and the *Faner* pile dwindle. *Y Cymro* is actually produced in England, in Oswestry, by its editor, Llion Griffiths, and a staff of three. 'We are sure that we get extra satisfaction from working in the Welsh language,' the editor said. 'In a way it is working for a cause and the language is the extra ingredient that makes it all worthwhile.'

Part of the Welsh language movement – and how large a part is difficult to say – is fuelled by a belief in 'the Welsh way of life', a concept based partly in fact, but is also a dream, a hope and a myth. The expression was coined about thirty-five years ago and although its definition remains rather loose it is a piece of shorthand, a codeword that many thousands of people in Wales understand without difficulty. It means a kind of life lived by literate, democratic, classless, Welsh-speaking country communities. It was identified and romanticized by people like Sir O. M. Edwards and, later, it became a fundamental part of nationalist philosophy. It is a Welsh way of life, certainly, but not *the* Welsh way of life. The concept seems to have little relevance to many people in the industrial society in south-east Wales, even if it is understood; and valleys people would say: 'Isn't our way of life – non-Welsh-language though it is – just as important a Welsh way of life?' And, year by year, the reality in the Welsh way of life is being steadily eroded, while the romance and hope and belief which are the very stuff of it, seem to exert an increasingly powerful attraction. The defence of the Welsh way of life, the defence of the language, in effect, plays an important part in Welsh politics; and the burning of the bombing school in Lleyn by three leading nationalists, in 1936, and the sabotage that followed the drowning of the Tryweryn valley in the nineteen-sixties, were acts done in the name of the Welsh way of life.

When people talk of the Welsh way of life, they usually have in their minds a community like Llanuwchllyn, which lies between the Aran mountain and Bala Lake, in Merioneth. Although only an hour's drive from the English border it has remained utterly Welsh and has kept a grip on the sort of priorities and values that had vanished in most of rural England forty or fifty years ago, and have been crumbling in much of rural Wales these past twenty years. It has seven hundred people, three nonconformist chapels, a church, an inn, a school, a post office–store, a grocery shop, several graveyards, a garage, a hall, a carpenter–undertaker and a village policeman. There are about sixty farms in the district and the people work on the land, in the forests, in the local creamery and in the schools and offices of Bala and Dolgellau. Although depopulation is a long-term problem there is no unemployment in the village and no one is poor. In the general election of October 1974 all but thirty of the five hundred and twenty people on the voters' list went to the poll, and the majority of them voted for *Plaid Cymru*. Most of the people have allegiance to a chapel even if they are no longer regular attenders. Almost all of them live their lives through Welsh and do not need to use English much. On Sunday the village pub, the Eagles, is closed because Merioneth voted in the last Sunday-opening referendum to stay 'dry'. And when you walk around Llanuwchllyn on a Sunday you do not hear the noise of car-washing, lawnmowing and power-drilling that you would hear in England. The Sunday sound of Llanuwchllyn is peace.

But it would be wrong to conclude that the village is dull, repressed and under the chapel thumb. On the contrary, Llanuwchllyn must rank as one of the culturally wealthiest villages in all Britain. The weekday sound is of laughter, music and debate, because the village has a tradition of busily creative self-entertainment and, in 1974, won the award of the national *eisteddfod* for being the most culturally active in Wales. It has seven drama groups, seven choirs, five well-known poets and a sprinkling of minor ones. It also has a pop group. The local *eisteddfod* has a reputation for high standards, the hall is always packed and, often, it does not finish until two o'clock in the morning. Sideboards gleam with *eisteddfod* trophies. A collection of the work of prize-winning local poets, which is published every year, sells over a thousand copies. The village hall is the most-used in Merioneth and is booked every night for meetings, rehearsals, debates and the word-battles between poets and wits that are so popular in rural Wales. At the height of the culture season, from harvest thanksgiving to St David's Day, men come home from work and ask 'What's on tonight?' and they do not mean television. There are busy branches of the Welsh youth league, of the Women's Institute and of *Merched y Wawr*, the Welsh-language women's movement. There is a gardeners' club, too. There is little gambling in Llanuwchllyn – even if they had the inclination it seems that most people would not be able to find the time – and the majority get no closer to the devil in this respect than to take part in the *twrnamaint draffts* and the *gyrfa chwist*, the whist drive.

The village school provides the sort of imaginative and small-class education that many parents would envy. There are about seventy children, aged four to eleven, taught by a headmaster and four teachers, and from an early age they have close contact with poetry and music, and they all have the chance to learn the harp. This district is in the heartland of *penillion*, the singing of verse to the harp.

Llanuwchllyn shows off its home-grown cultural wealth at its own *eisteddfod* and at many others. It is never shown off as a folklore exhibition for tourists. In this village culture is not for sale, not a commodity dished out: it is lived. For this reason it is difficult for many of the villagers to comprehend the anxiety often expressed elsewhere about the condition of Welsh. After all, their Welsh way of life is as natural to them as food and sleep and they might not speak English from one week to the next. But that is a false security. The threats, even to this busy and strong community, are plain enough. An Anglesey man who moved into the village said that Llanuwchllyn was like the Anglesey of a quarter of a century ago, thoroughly Welsh. 'But go to Anglesey now and look at the extent of immigration from England. See how the place has deteriorated culturally.'

To comprehend the threats to Llanuwchllyn we must examine its strengths. There are four main reasons why it has remained closely knit, fertile, contented and Welsh. It has deep roots, the chapel has remained comparatively strong, it has community leadership and it has been able to absorb the thin trickle of English immigration. Many of the people live in houses that have been in their families for two centuries and more, and they are branches of a few great families. So Llanuwchllyn is a community of cousins, and funerals, therefore, tend to be large gatherings. One of the ministers said he had stopped the practice of reading out the names of all the people related to someone who had died, because it took too much time. An Englishman driving through the village was stopped to allow a funeral procession to pass. Fuming, he counted seventy-six cars and remarked caustically that it was the largest funeral he had seen since Winston Churchill's. One of the significant changes in village life during the past decade has been the fall in chapel attendance and the increase in pub attendance. The Rev. W. J. Edwards, the Congregationalist minister, said that many people still used the chapel, but a lot tended to come in for choir practice and not for the services. All over the Welsh countryside community leaders are wondering whether the shrinking of chapel influence is leading to a withering of the culture's roots. They admit that Welsh is lively in many respects and has found new expression, but they say that Welsh speech and literature owes much of their high standards and vigour to the chapels which have been centres of education and appreciation of literature and music, as well as places of worship. There is concern that the Welsh spoken by many young people is losing its old majesty and is on the way to becoming an argot, full of slipshod constructions and jargon. Welsh-speaking, but what sort of Welsh? Posters advertising a rally put on by a political splinter group were riddled with errors, and posters for a pop concert had almost as many mistakes as words. Young people, however, point out that they care deeply for the language and that they have struggled and suffered for it in a way their elders did not; and they add that the inns were always the centre of village life before the chapels took power. A young man said: 'We love our culture and we respect the chapel. We just like a pint and see no harm in it.'

Meanwhile there is the question of the *tai haf*. It has been estimated that four out of ten homes in the north Wales countryside will be second homes by the end of the century. In the Llanuwchllyn district forty houses that, twenty years ago, were the homes of Welsh-speaking families, are now *tai haf* or are derelict. So far the numbers of English people who have settled permanently, occupying fewer than a dozen houses in the village, have been too small to offer a threat to the cultural and linguistic integrity of the place, or have been absorbed to a greater or smaller extent. But all around are examples of communities reduced to husks by the combined effects of depopulation, second-home ownership and local government carelessness. For many people in rural Wales the word anglicization has come to mean corrosion. 'What we worry about is a continuing pressure from second-home seekers, and we are afraid that someone might get permission to build an estate of houses which could be a nucleus of non-Welsh-speaking people,' Mr Edwards, the minister, said. 'This has nothing to do with xenophobia; anyone will tell you that we are a welcoming and hospitable community. But what we have can be so easily undermined, and in rural Wales the wedges are being hammered in all the time.'

Not many English settlers in the Welsh countryside have seen much purpose in integrating linguistically and culturally, although there are signs that attitudes are changing now. 'The trouble is that it takes only one English-speaker to change the language of a meeting,' Mr Ifor Owen, the headmaster of Llanuwchllyn's school, said. 'Because we are a polite and sociable people we will readily change the language to make a newcomer feel welcome. Perhaps Welshmen have been too polite for the health of the language. Once a nucleus of non-Welsh-speakers is established in a small community the Welsh language is on the defensive. It is always we who have built the bridges out to the English-speakers. They have rarely built bridges out to us.'

Still, some settlers are sensitive enough to recognize that they have moved into a different culture and are prepared to build bridges. Even if they find linguistic integration difficult themselves they see to it that their children fit into the culture. When Carol and Terry Parmenter moved from

Woolwich to Llanuwchllyn they made a considerable cultural and social step. Their boys attend the village school and have fluent Welsh. Mr Parmenter said that Wales was a foreign land, and that was the spice of life. 'The best things about the village are the schooling and the community life. The people here are kind and concerned and everyone says hello, which is something you don't get in cities. And at election times you have proper conversations with people who call round, even if you don't agree with their politics. The boys love school and are having the sort of schooling we never even dreamed of. We are proud they speak Welsh so well and knowing another language broadens their minds. I suppose we had our doubts at first about the boys going to a Welsh-language school, but they took to it so easily and we don't have any worries at all. Let me show you my eldest boy's report: Welsh reading, nine and a half out of ten; English reading, nine and a half out of ten; total marks ninety-three and half out of a hundred. And he's still only second! It may be a funny thing for a Londoner to say, but because of the importance of the language and the way the boys get on in school, we would not like to uproot ourselves now. I'll be frank and admit that sometimes the language gets under my skin. I wish they would say a few words in English at the school concert just to keep us in the picture. But it's their country, isn't it, and it's their language, and you can see why they want to keep it.'

For all its vitality and apparent strength, Llanuwchllyn is vulnerable and even fragile. Like other strong communities it is both beacon and well; but the threats are real enough and, like many another Llan, it could be wrecked in a generation.

I write at a time of significant growth in Welsh confidence and consciousness, and of greater interest in the fortunes of Welsh than at any time in its history. And there is naturally a relation between these developing strands. It is not too difficult to explain the language revival; it is a reaction against uniformity, centralization and the dehumanizing aspects of the advance of our kind of civilization. It is an effort to keep a hold on heritage, to keep a myth intact; a struggle against being dispossessed. Given the stubbornness of human beings and their priorities, it is an inevitable struggle. And although it has its particles of hypocrisy, foolishness, tedium and over-zealousness, and although it might be doomed, it is a healthy thing.

Of course, there is impatience at this revival. 'Kicking a dying horse ... they can all speak English anyway.' But I would say, and there is some statistical evidence to support this, that the majority of people in Wales are willing that those who want to live through Welsh should do so, and that Welsh should have the official support it needs. Many non-Welsh-speakers take a pleasure and pride in the language's existence.

On the other hand, most of those who do not have Welsh do not want it to intrude too much into their lives. They begin to bristle if it becomes an inconvenience. They do not think that the language is the pre-eminent political issue that some leading language campaigners say it is. Nor do they think that Welsh is the only badge of Welsh identity. They look at their valley homes where community spirit, loyalty and socialism are prime constituents, where there are distinctive attitudes, accents and characteristics, shaped by history and environments, and they ask: 'Who could be more Welsh than us?'

But there is a need for more opportunities for the non-Welsh-speaking majority to express their Welshness – and Cardiff Arms Park is not enough. There is a need, too, for wider understanding of Welsh Wales in English Wales. The non-Welsh-speaker needs more information about his neighbour and much of the responsibility lies with education authorities, with teachers, journalists and broadcasters; and also with government and local government who can do more to create the conditions for social harmony. Communicators, for instance, have been too preoccupied with confrontation as 'good television' and 'good copy' and could play a more constructive role in the interpretation of Welsh Wales and English Wales, one to the other. By now we should be moving out of the period of inane bickering over the two languages and the squealing at infringements of trivial 'rights', real and imagined, that have characterized so many newspaper letters, and discussions on the air and in the bar. Because Wales does not yet have a great enough sense of solidarity, of unity, or enough information, there is some intolerance and tension. There is, for example, a suspicion, occasionally articulated by politicians and councillors, that Welsh-speakers are keeping the best jobs for themselves in education, broadcasting, local government and other public services. But the concept of a Welsh-speaking Mafia doing Welsh boys out of jobs has no foundation. Complaints are often rooted in rumour and prejudice and in the occasional disappointment of unsuccessful applicants for posts, who blame their lack of Welsh. In reality, for the great majority of Welsh people, the language offers no obstacle to progress in their careers. With perhaps a few exceptions the jobs that are advertised with a Welsh-essential tag are jobs that people without Welsh could not do. Teaching is a profession said by outsiders to have its Welsh Mafia element and, of course, thousands of teaching jobs in Welsh-speaking areas require Welsh. But the teachers' union is satisfied that there is no Mafia and that opportunities to reach the top are equal for all, Welsh-speaking or not. In local government and public services there are comparatively few jobs where Welsh is essential and the extent of Welsh-speaking in these and many other fields naturally reflects the language pattern as a whole. It is fair to say that if there really were discrimination on language grounds, trade unions and professional bodies would be quick to complain. The other aspect of this question is that there are jobs that can be done only, or done best, by bilingual people. It seems to me important that Welsh has an economic value because I find it difficult to believe that a language could survive without that. People who say that there is no point in continuing to teach Welsh on the ground that it is 'useless and won't get you a job' are often the same people who complain when they see that it is not, and that it will. This is sensitive territory, where belief and prejudice can easily clash. There is a strong argument for trying to increase the number of jobs where the ability to speak Welsh is an asset, but you cannot pursue that course without involving and informing the English-speaking majority: the development of Welsh requires their co-operation. Employers could do more in this field by advertising many Welsh-essential posts with the offer to send otherwise suitable applicants on language courses. The Gwynedd county council, which has a bilingual policy, already does this; and, as I have written earlier, some employers, in commerce as well as public service, are sending men to intensive language courses.

The business world could do more for the language in other ways. Official support is vital and helps to take heat out of the issue because it is a seal of approval and help to make Welsh what it should be: normal, everyday and unremarkable. But only one of the banks, the Midland, offers a bilingual service as a matter of routine and very few shops and stores, even in the Welsh heartlands, make use of the language in displays and on signs and tickets; they really should be making a greater contribution.

As attitudes to the Welsh language change, the question of how Welsh should live alongside English is now discussed more broadly. Part of the language movement is to give Welsh more toeholds, a justified existence in science and technology as well as the arts. The view that Welsh is only a language of the hearth has become outdated. A strong thread of the new consciousness is the effort being made to use Welsh in those areas of work and expression where English was formerly regarded as the only practical medium. Because the language has not been used much in certain fields it has lacked words and jargon, particularly of a technical kind. And to meet the modern demand for new terms there has been a steady stream of glossaries. The growing use of Welsh in the courts, for example, led to the compilation of a book of legal terms: it has been invaluable in the training of interpreters, judges, magistrates, solicitors and barristers and clerks whose purpose is to make the use of Welsh in the courts a routine and unremarkable right, in the spirit of the Welsh Language Act.

There are also glossaries covering economics, mathematics, public health, office administration, biology, sport, cuisine and geography. Some of the terms are specially coined, others are disused words that have been revived. In

1975 the Academi Cymreig, the Welsh Academy, commissioned a new English–Welsh dictionary, to corral all the technical terms and modern expressions and to stimulate further the process of working new terms into the mainstream of the language through broadcasting, discussion, books and journals. Welsh-speakers are often criticized for failing to use Welsh terms enough and for peppering their talk with English technical expressions. Meanwhile, a group of doctors, both GPs and consultants, founded an association of Welsh-speaking doctors to further the use of Welsh in medicine; and the British Medical Association supported the principle that non-Welsh-speaking doctors appointed to Welsh-speaking areas should be given leave and expenses to attend language courses.

One thing that is missing in the debate, the struggling and wrangling over Welsh and what is to be done about it, is some old-fashioned tact. A woman who was learning Welsh and had become fairly fluent was talking with a university lecturer, and seemed to be getting on well. But after a while he demolished her abruptly by saying: 'Your past tenses are awful.' And moved off to speak to someone else. A teacher in a bilingual school was talking to a couple about their child; the father was a Welsh-speaker, the mother not. When the mother asked a question the teacher replied only to the father, in Welsh. In south Wales, councillors voted against giving a new street a Welsh name, admitting they did so because nationalists had won a few seats on the council. There are numerous examples of similar tactlessness and bigotry. The perpetrators are fools because tension is to a large extent the sum of all the little grains of foolishness, thoughtlessness and prejudice.

The Welsh revival has a fair head of steam, but the number of Welsh-speakers continues to fall. Perhaps, at the 1981 census, the total may be under half a million. But the revival may have begun in time; the nursery schools might prove as important in this century as the chapels were in the past. And attitudes are changing. I think that the efforts being made to keep the pulse of Welsh strong are important not only for the reasons of identity and heritage that piston the broad language movement, but also because it has a bearing on English. The very forces that make up a considerable part of the threat to Welsh also endanger English, a language increasingly shot through with jargon, obfuscation and the claptrap of non-communication, a language losing its strength, elegance and distinctiveness. It may be curious, but there is a sense in which the movement for Welsh is also a movement for English.

CHAPTER FIVE

A Comb Through the Celtic Fringe

The national *eisteddfod* of Wales had been wrapped up and put away for another year and, still feeling the effects of its life-giving vapours, a large invading force of Welsh, about three hundred and fifty men and women, were bound for the international Celtic congress, the yearly corroboree of the Celtic fragments of north-west Europe. They set off in coaches adorned with dragon flags and badges. There were some cans of ale, in case of emergency, and the invaders sang from north Wales to the south, from the south down to Southampton, across the English Channel, and then from Cherbourg to Nantes, the old capital of Brittany. Here they met up with a platoon of Scots, a raiding party of Irish, a fistful of Cornishmen and a brace or two of Manx – and, of course, a great battalion of Bretons. I did not travel with the Welsh contingent. I went independently by car, as befits a man who values his freedom of movement for professional reasons and his impartial status. I also went by a different and more circuitous route, as befits a man who leaves his travel arrangements to someone else. It is more than four hundred miles from Calais to Nantes and I arrived at the university, the congress venue, at two o'clock in the morning.

The sleepy *concierge* at the hall of residence handed me my key.

'*Où sont les Gallois?*' I inquired.

He mobilized one prawn-like eyebrow.

'*Monsieur?*'

'*Les Gallois.*'

The *concierge* flicked his eyebrow in the direction of the building across the square and I was suddenly aware of a well-worn old hymn floating gently in the warm air.

Calon lan yn llawn daioni,
Tecach yw na'r lili dlos . . .

'*Les Gallois,*' the *concierge* said.

The singing, naturally enough at that time of the morning, was the work of the younger section of the Welsh contingent; and it was young people who significantly altered the tone of a congress that was first held in 1895, at a time when there was a growth of interest in Celtic matters, and which has had for many years the highly respectable and rather genteel image of the middle-aged having a scholarly prod at their Celtic roots. 'Very pleasant, but with a tendency to be all harps and clogs dances,' said one congress-goer.

This congress in Nantes, however, had a distinctly youthful and political tone. The middle-aged Celts were still there all right, but they were augmented by large and vigorous groups of young men and women, bright as popinjays in tee shirts, and assertive, too, declaring that the small cultures they were born into are worth keeping and worth struggling for. They seemed determined to involve themselves in the struggle. 'We are responsible people. We want to guard the wealth and pass it on,' a young man said.

For the Welsh the congress was, in parts, a sort of overseas edition of the *eisteddfod*. And everything ran by Celtic time. That is, if you arrived an hour late for an event, you were still half an hour early. You could hear, if you listened carefully, seven languages. Welsh, Breton, Irish, Scots, Gaelic, and even Cornish and Manx. But, ironically, much of the business had to be conducted through those vehicles of destructive mass culture, French and English.

The Welsh quickly formed a choir on their arrival, not because they wanted to live out a cliché, but because every national group was asked to contribute to the programme in a congress concert . . . and the Welsh were asked to form a choir and give a performance of the power-singing for which they are noted. In their late-night rehearsals the singers appeared to be using *vin rouge* as a throat spray. Indeed, the Welsh seemed to be more liberated than the others, perhaps because Wales, unlike Ireland and Brittany, is now going through a largely post-Christian age, perhaps because there is a deeply rooted exuberance in thè Welsh soul that puritanism never flushed out completely. On the other hand, traditions die hard and most Welsh people have proper sensibilities, and Sunday would not be Sunday without a chapel service; so a nonconformist minister was shipped over from Wales to conduct one. I thought that the Bretons got on particularly well with the Welsh. The Bretons were an enthusiastic lot with a tendency to jump up at the drop of a Gauloise and link arms and do a gavotte to an insistent rhythm; this clearly satisfied a basic need, and the Welsh seemed to understand this. In the same way, the Bretons seemed to understand the Welsh need to break into song and dig hard for the harmonies. The Scots got on well with the Irish and kept a wary eye on their more exuberant, and more numerous, fellow-Celts. They did not care much for all the talk in the conference sessions for political action to save the Celtic languages, and spoke in businesslike tones of the benefits of 'working quietly from within'. There was a lot of serious talking in the conference hall, an exploration of the common problems, but, as I say, it was not all serious. Suddenly, at lunch or dinner, a dozen Bretons would spring to their feet, chanting rhythmically. As their fellows beat time with spoons on the tables, they would link their brown arms and jig sideways in piquant Celtic conga. Their cousin-Celts would chew on, unperturbed and happily tolerant, and with no wish to join the exhibition. But at night, in the large square of the romantic Château des Ducs de Bretagne, to the supernatural sound of pipe and horn, everybody would link arms and gavotte and shuffle together in the electric unity of tribalism. Were they dancing in their own twilight?

They would answer, emphatically, no.

If you are pessimistic you might conclude that the weight of evidence is that the Celts are making a last gallant wave of the arm as the quicksand closes over. Certainly the Celtic revival is a fascinating phenomenon, a many-faceted mixture of the sentimental and the spiritual, the digging in of a minority's heels, a shout against the relentlessly rolling leviathan of mass culture and uniformity and totalitarianism; a fist against philistinism, and also a kick against the remoteness, incompetence, theorizing and anti-provincialism of centralized rule. The Celts have been offered total absorption into mass culture, or have been pressured into it; and most have accepted the situation. But a minority do not want their own cultures to shrink and die so that the bones can be prodded in peace by academics in the centuries to come. The shout is the human one: let us survive. It is pointless to say, as critics of the revival do, that the world is no worse off because sailors roasted all the dodos. The Celts have dug into their half-buried past and have retrieved their legends and the missing links of their collective personalities, and they can see more clearly where they stand in history and in relation to modern cultural and political developments. Celtic feeling can be very powerful indeed, and writers sometimes imbue it with mystery and hint at deep significance, but the essence of Celtic awareness today is that the Celts are like most people: they would rather be alive than dead, and they want to be alive as Celts.

There can be no doubt that the Celts are making their last stand. As distinct peoples they have been for two thousand years a bright thread in the evolution of European civilization. Now they have reached the ultimate crisis in their long march and decline. They are not a relic. They are a tough remnant. And by the end of this century it will be possible to judge whether they have gouged out for themselves a worthwhile and valid future – or have been effectively erased by the progress to which they have contributed much.

The definition of the term Celtic is beset by conflicting considerations, but I agree with the view that the term is primarily a linguistic one and that the quintessential distinguishing mark of a Celt is his possession of a native Celtic language. It can be estimated that more than one and a half million people speak – use daily and ordinarily – Welsh, Irish, Breton and Gaelic. There are more than half a million Welsh-speakers, seventy thousand Irish-speakers, eighty thousand Gaelic-speakers, and perhaps three-quarters of a million Breton-speakers. Cornish and Manx are, to my mind, dead languages. It is difficult to generalize about the Celtic languages and some generalizations seem absurd if you include Cornish and Manx in them, so these remarks about Celtic languages apply essentially to Welsh and Breton, Irish and Gaelic. The last native Cornish speaker died more than a century and a half ago, but a growth of interest in the language has led to the development of a nucleus of perhaps two or three hundred people who can read, write and even speak Cornish. There are people who dream of a restoration of Cornish as a widely-spoken language, but that would seem to be as likely as the reconnection of a severed head. In saying that, however, I do not underestimate the strength of Cornish feeling and the gradual growth of awareness in Cornwall of a Celtic heritage and identity. Although Cornwall's Celtic fire died down long ago a handful of people are blowing hard on the embers. A Cornish *gorsedd* of bards has existed for fifty years, there are occasionally church services in Cornish – a few couples have been married in Cornish in recent years – and there is a slowly growing volume of poetry and stories being published in the old language, and this fills a large gap because Cornish never had a substantial literature. There are other manifestations of Cornishness, too: a nationalist movement that fights at Parliamentary elections and has won a few local authority seats; and an attempt to revive the ancient Stannary Parliament, the senate of the Cornish tin miners, once the main legislature of Cornwall. As for the Manx language, it is learned by a small group of enthusiasts and has a small ceremonial role, but no genuine existence. The distinguishing mark of Man today is the birch with which they beat boys.

All of the four main Celtic languages are in crisis. If they all succumb – that is, if they shrivel to a point where their use is minimal and artificial, and they cannot regenerate – the Celts, the last of those colourful and cultured and gifted people who were the original Britons, may be said to have vanished. They would leave a vast literature and a mythology, great monuments and the husks of languages, folk memories and aches, and a complete human experience, with a beginning, middle and an anguished end.

A Breton-speaker remarked to me, in a gloomy moment: 'I'm afraid that we are the Red Indians of Europe. We are squeezed out because we do not fit the scheme of things in the modern civilized world with its emphasis on efficiency at all costs and centralist control. We are reduced to picturesque oddities with an imposed vocation for tourism as we live out our last years.

'And if we kick against this situation and say to our governments: Look, we believe our cultures are worth helping and they should have some economic and administrative help, some schools for the little ones and the kind of official recognition that helps to build a wall against contempt – what happens? We get a polite smile. But the really sad thing is that the greatest enmity and the deepest apathy is found among our own people. A small culture requires a lot of care and patience, and tolerance, too; but today's world is the world of the short cut, the quick results, entertainment on tap. People tend to measure a minority language in francs.'

Whether the erosion, leading to death, of the remaining Celtic languages represents an ethnic tragedy is a matter of personal outlook. It may be, as some people contend, that concern for minor languages and their cultures is a mixture of sentiment and ancestor worship, a pointless battling against the inevitable, both a waste of time and a waste of money, an aspect of arid nationalism, a narrow and possibly dangerous preoccupation with something useless in a world where the enormous problems of economics and unemployment, strife and intolerance, predominate.

In any case, the world has five thousand languages. How important is the loss of a few? If it comes to that – how important is the loss of a few hundred? Who cares now that great languages, peoples, civilizations have been swept away in history's torrent? Wouldn't international intercourse be easier if five thousand languages were steadily reduced to, say, half a dozen?

To other people this seems to be a cynical and cold outlook. It reduces language to a code of symbols and sounds used only for bald communication, like Morse and Esperanto. It ignores the power and mystery of language, its grip on men's personalities, its role as ethnic cement and carapace, its part in collective identity, culture and history.

Language is much more than a code; and the recognition of its fundamental qualities is at the heart of the Celtic revival and the resistance to pressures threatening the Celtic languages. I know that it is difficult for people to comprehend the noises-off, particularly from Wales, and to be convinced that they are anything more than extremism and the dying twitches of useless tongues. It should be accepted, however, that while a handful of professional angry young men will leap to the support of the nearest minority cause, most of the people involved in, or sympathetic to, language movements, believe they are working for something of great value, a compound of beauty, pleasure and identity, the transmission of history and of thought, the saving of their own communities and the stockades where they can refresh themselves.

In all the Celtic countries there is great awareness that the forces of economics, electronics, mass tourism and the wealth of opportunities at the centres, now combine into a deadly corrosive to attack the minority languages where centuries of outlawing, repression and ridicule succeeded only partly. The enemy, an Irish scholar said to me in Dublin, is the uniformity of material culture which is hostile to distinctiveness and leads to ethnicide, the elimination of distinctive cultures.

While the causes of the erosion of the Celtic languages are much the same in each case, there are certain important differences, and resistance to the threats is neither concerted nor uniform. Also, each language lives in a situation different from that of its cousin-languages.

The Breton language, for example, has no status and has been largely repressed under the long-standing centralist policies of France. Officially, it does not exist, and because Breton-speakers are not counted in administrative returns, it is difficult to say with any accuracy how many speak it. In 1970 people who studied Breton affairs talked of a million speakers, but many estimates now run to three-quarters of a million or less, and most of them are in the older generation. The language has only a toehold in mass communications and education. For more than seventy years it was prohibited in the schools, but is now taught to secondary school pupils – outside school hours and providing there is a willing teacher available. I went to a village in Brittany where teachers were at a summer school improving their knowledge of the language and Breton history. When I arrived they were clustered around a radio set. The attraction was not so much the programme itself as the fact that it was actually in Breton. 'The government gives us all concessions on radio and television,' one of the teachers said. 'It throws straws to the drowning man.' Twice a week there is a ninety-second Breton 'spot' on local television, but Breton speakers complain that the time is so short that the announcer has to gabble and is not easy to understand. Still, there is a twenty-minute Breton magazine programme; it goes out twice a month at one-thirty p.m. A French minister of education once said: *Pour l'unité linguistique de la France, la langue Bretonne doit disparaître.'** And France's policy, or, rather, non-policy where Breton is concerned has brought the language to within a few years of vanishing as a widely-spoken one. That may seem a strong statement, considering that up to a third of Brittany's three million people are Breton-speakers, and that Breton is the largest Celtic language, but the language has been attacked at the root. It has no institutions, a fundamental requirement. It has had no worthwhile place in education for more than ninety years, so that most Breton-speakers cannot read or write the language. In Wales, the translation of the Bible into Welsh and the growth of the chapels led to a widespread literacy in Welsh. But Breton had no Bible lifeline. In the past thirty years, however, a growing number of people have developed a modern Breton literature, but some of them remain pessimistic about the future. 'It is true that public attitudes are beginning to change,' one of the teachers said. 'Until recently most Breton parents tended to avoid using the language in front of their children so that the use of French – the language of getting on in the world – was encouraged. And Breton was always snubbed and degraded. You'll still see plenty of evidence of that, but more people today are becoming aware that they are losing something of value to them. But we have to be realistic. There are very few young

* 'For French linguistic unity, Breton must disappear.'

Breton-speakers and when Bretons meet to discuss ways of saving the language they have to speak in French a good deal because not everyone at the meeting understands Breton. In Wales, you see, people are fighting to hold on to what they have, but Bretons are trying to get back what they have lost. We read with interest about the struggle for the Welsh language because it gives us heart. But if Bretons had only a fraction of what the Welsh have in the way of radio and television programmes, in government support and educational support, we would think that a crazy dream had come true.'

The Bretons envy the official status of the Irish language. Article Eight of the republic's constitution says it is the first and national language – as befits the former fuel of Irish nationalism. It is compulsory in the schools; there are bilingual signs and forms and up to twenty-seven per cent of Ireland's 2,800,000 people are said to be Irish-speaking. This all looks fine in theory. But in practice Irish is the subject of a rescue operation and is a language on the dole. It has a genuine existence only in the communities of the Gaeltacht, the remote and precious Irish-speaking fringes of the west, and south, of Galway, Mayo, Donegal, Cork, Kerry, Meath and Waterford. The Gaeltacht population is now only seventy thousand, a thin thread to hang on to. The economic problems of these areas are serious and the young stream away to find work. The Gaeltacht is being kept alive economically because it is the last natural spring of the language. Government agencies are trying to stem the outward tide by providing work, supporting small established industries and attracting new ones. The state-sponsored Gaeltacht development board says there is no intention to create an Irish 'reservation' because that would be insulting and futile, and it regards the Gaeltacht as a nucleus, not an island. Nevertheless, development in a region that is fast losing its young people is a race against time.

Scottish Gaelic is confined to the islands and the Highlands of the west – with the exception of a body of Gaelic speakers in Glasgow – and is spoken by eighty thousand people. Its official status is meagre and its government support is not strong, although a few agencies do worthwhile work in promoting it through books, pamphlets and lessons. In some schools it is well taught, and it is also served by a few radio programmes and by some writers and publishers. But many Gaelic-speakers are apathetic and although some young Gaels are well aware that apathy is an important element in language decay and have formed a language ginger group, the long-term prospects for Gaelic are uncertain.

So, the stubborn Celtic languages, clinging to the rocky edges of the north-west of Europe, are dwindling. And, in the end, do many people care? It has to be said that there is considerable indifference to their fate and this is shared even by many of the people who speak them.

The critics of language campaigns often deny that language is necessarily involved in the question of identity. The opponents of Irish language policy say, for example, 'nobody doubts that we are Irishmen, and distinctive, regardless of vernacular'. An English-speaking Scot surely feels Scottish and may not have heard a word of Gaelic in his life; many Bretons feel Breton, rather than French, although they have been cut off from their native language; and people clearly feel Welsh without having the Welsh language. In my view, the non-language distinctiveness is usually fragile and quite vague and likely to become more so as uniform culture spreads. In any case, the speaker of the Celtic language is the one who stands to lose most and, should he feel sincerely that national identity and small-language culture are important values that would perish with the death of the spoken language, his feelings should surely be respected, even if they cannot be shared.

A lively Celtic Congress leaves all who go there very hopeful about the future of their particular cultures. Of course, the fortunes of language can alter, but unless there are radical changes it is difficult to see how Breton, Irish and Scottish Gaelic can survive in the long term as everyday community languages, and not just the minority interest of relatively few students and academics.

The Welsh situation is different from the others and although the language retreats. Wales is very much the cockpit of Celtic resistance. Here the intensity of the determination to save the language is stronger. Indeed, of all the Celtic languages Welsh is the one through which the last of the Celts are most likely to have a distinct existence well into the twenty-first century.

There is much serious talking done at Celtic congresses, and so there was at Nantes, but the event was not especially gloomy. On the contrary, there was generous time allowed for singing, dancing and a general letting down of hair. There was also a festival of religious songs and music in a church presented by the various Celtic nations. The Welsh contribution was a *penillion* singer, a small group of girl singers and a mighty choir which apparently consisted of any Welsh person who entered the place. Trying to retain my impartial status, I sought a seat away from the centre of the action, but was waylaid by one of the choral press gang.

'Tenor or bass?' he challenged.

Having a singing capability unjudged outside my bathroom walls, I said I had no idea and in the best traditions of journalism tried to make an excuse and leave. But my way was blocked by a medieval pillar and some choir heavies. The press-gang captain looked me over without enthusiasm. 'Well, tenors are taller than basses, and basses have bigger chests than tenors. You must be a tenor.' He directed me to the tenor seats and I embarked upon a new experience – the membership of a Welsh choir giving a gala performance in a foreign land. I could say, hereafter, with pride unalloyed with modesty, that I had sung for Wales. I told the man in the next seat that I feared I could not sing at all within the real meaning of the word, and that I had not been in a choir since I was a surpliced angel of eleven singing for brides for one-and-six and for corpses for one-and-nine and reading the *Beano* during the sermons. He was not perturbed. 'Don't worry. The secret of singing in a mass choir is to open your mouth wide and look intelligent.' He handed me a hymn sheet. 'I'm sure you can open your mouth.' Another man said: 'The secret of singing in a Welsh choir is to find a man who can sing on pitch and stand very close to him. At first you will be three-quarters of a beat behind him, but you should aim in the long run to be no more than a quarter of a beat behind.'

The concert opened with Breton horn players, in tiny

sentry boxes high up in the church gallery, playing plaintive, reedy elvish tunes, evocative of legends, mysteries and druidic rites in wild remote Celtic places. Then they played some more and the Irish came on with fiddles and whistles followed by some Welsh girls whose singing remained utterly composed and beautiful while French television technicians and film crews ducked and weaved around them like playful gibbons, placing microphones within a millimetre of their lips and gesticulating to each other in silent frenzy while directors, all corduroy and beads, grimaced and mouthed instructions. The Breton horn players blew a fresh fusillade of faerie fanfares; there was more song, and the Breton pipers piped again. The Welsh began to grow restless, like rugby forwards impatient for the ball to be thrown into the scrum, as they waited to launch their hymns on the air. The horns' sound died away at last. We were on. The conductor spread his arms wide, and the music struck up and we opened the roaring sluices of song as the film cameras came homing in for those shots of dental fillings, trembling tonsils and flaring nostrils that are the very stuff of *ciné vérité*. I sang most of the hymns, and there were many sung that evening, and tried to keep no more than three-quarters of a beat behind my companions. We ended with a great finale of sound and emotion and the Breton horn players rounded it all off with just one more burst. With the music ringing in our ears we spilled out into the warm night.

Later, there was gavotting in a café and we shuffled round and round the tables, linked by arms and warm tribal feeling. A policeman came to investigate the source of the noise, took one look and hurried off, shaking his head. Next evening, the gavotte was still there: it seemed to have become a permanent feature of life, a roundabout you could ride and dismount as you wished. For a while I shared a table with three Breton women and we ate winkles and long bread and drank Muscadet, the wine of the region, and talked for a long time about *les problèmes Celtiques*. We gavotted as the mood took us. It was well into the small hours when the drooping proprietor called a halt. The gavotte, however, did not stop and we watched a crowd of people dance and shuffle and chant away down the dark street, a rhythmic centipede, towards the floodlit Château des Ducs de Bretagne. The three girls planted an *au revoir* kiss on each cheek, and I reciprocated, feeling like de Gaulle at an investiture. They melted away and I, thrice double-kissed and content with wine and winkles, walked beneath the stars with the rhythm of the dance and a snatch of Breton pipe tune rattling around my skull like a train on the Circle Line.

CHAPTER SIX

Body Politic

There is no such thing as Welsh politics, a leading politician said to me once. But the evidence is that, increasingly during the decade from the mid-nineteen-sixties to the mid-seventies, Wales became a separate arena in the politics of Britain as national consciousness grew and confidence in the ability of London to manage Welsh affairs declined. Indeed, the decade was marked by an astonishing flowering of the regional dimension in British politics. In the general election of 1966 the Labour party held thirty-two of the thirty-six Welsh seats, and more than three-fifths of the vote, and could claim to be, in most respects, the national party of Wales. A Labour MP remarked that south Wales, in particular, was a one-party democracy. In local government Labour was the establishment, so secure that most councillors were not concerned with the problems of gaining or retaining power; large majorities were taken for granted and councillors were preoccupied with the exercise of power. But the elements, and some of the machinery, for change were there: Labour had founded the Welsh Office, admittedly with a limited range of action, and was seriously discussing the idea of an elected assembly for Wales. And within eight years of 1966 the axis had shifted dramatically. Labour's holding had fallen to twenty-three seats and under half the votes polled. The Conservatives now had eight, Plaid Cymru three and the Liberals two. The nationalists were beginning to offer a stronger challenge for local authority seats. The Welsh Office had won for itself a greater share of the administration of Wales and the way was being cleared towards an elected assembly to bring much more of the management of Wales into Welsh hands. Meanwhile the Secretary of State was setting up the Welsh

Development Agency to help run the economy more effectively, the greatest devolutionary step since the founding of the Welsh Office itself. It was altogether a sharply different and more stimulating picture.

As long ago as 1910 Keir Hardie called for the appointment of a Secretary of State for Wales, but it was not until the thirties that the idea was pursued in earnest. Chamberlain rejected it, saying that Welsh affairs were well looked after; and he also denied Wales parity with Scotland (which had its own department of state) on the ground that Scotland had a different legal system – exactly the same argument that politicians used forty years later to deny a Welsh assembly the same powers as a Scottish one. James Griffiths, MP for Llanelli, was a central figure in the movement to get a Welsh Office established, and from 1945 a number of small steps were taken towards the gaining of this necessary apparatus. One of the steps was an advisory council for Wales which attacked procrastination in the civil service and the lack of co-ordination among government departments operating in Wales. Enough people in the Labour party became converted to the concept of a Welsh Office, with a Cabinet minister for Wales, to have it put in the party manifestos in the 1959 and 1964 general elections. When Labour came to power in 1964 the promise was kept, and James Griffiths, fittingly in view of his patient work, became the first Secretary of State for Wales.

'We have been pressing for this major change for many years, as a mark of our national identity,' he said. 'This nation, with its distinctive traditions and language, could not feel at peace without the constitutional recognition that we have now gained.'

The establishment of the Welsh Office, and subsequent devolutionary measures, led to the discovery of a new feature of Welsh political geography. This was the slippery slope, a dangerous formation down which the Welsh people, who were not intelligent enough to assume some responsibility for managing their own affairs, were to be led, like Hamelin's children, to the abyss. As the years went by it became clear that the leaders were not just *Plaid* pipers, as some suggested, but were also in the Labour party and the

Liberal party in considerable strength; and were even in the Conservative party, too. Slowly, too slowly for some, they inched down the slope, finding that it was not so slippery after all, and saw, not an abyss, but a better and more efficient form of democratic government, bringing decision-making closer to the people and easing the legislative log-jam at Westminster.

At first the new Welsh Office, headquartered among the fine white buildings and shrubs of Cathays Park in Cardiff, had little devolved power. It had responsibility for local government, housing, planning and roads and a staff of two hundred. It had taken Welshmen a long time to prise open the tight fist of Whitehall and the tight eyelids of some politicians; and the struggle to wrest power from the civil service empire in Whitehall was to continue. For a time the Welsh Office had a distinctly colonial appearance: it had limited executive power, had to implement policies fashioned else-where and did not have the dignity of its own budget. White-hall's mandarins hoped that the Welsh Office would be a fairly small and tame creature, kept on a tight leash, but it gradually developed into a much larger animal. After ten years it had increased its staff sixfold and had responsibility for health, primary and secondary education, agriculture, as well as roads, housing and planning. It had become such a part of Welsh life that people wondered how they had got on without it. It rightly became a focus. But still its influence on policies, dictated by national considerations, was not strong enough for the liking of some politicians and civil servants in Wales. Whitehall's influence remained strong and there-fore was a source of frustration for Welsh Office staff and ministers who would have liked a budget better tailored to Welsh needs. The Treasury's tight and detailed costings ruled out the flexibility that the Welsh Office sought; and there was some public discontent with Welsh Office per-formance.

Meanwhile, the times were changing in Welsh politics. Significantly, the Welsh Labour party committed itself to the concept of an elected assembly to manage Welsh affairs, although some of the MPs did not like the idea. Then, in June 1966, forty-one years after its birth as a tiny band of language conservationists, *Plaid Cymru* won its first Parliamentary seat: Gwynfor Evans, the party's president, captured Carmarthen from Labour in a by-election. Labour called it a flash in the pan, but nine months later there was another flash, this time in Rhondda West, of all places, where *Plaid Cymru* came within two thousand votes of winning the by-election; and sixteen months after that there was another flash at Caerphilly where the nationalists cut a twenty-one thousand Labour majority to under two thousand.

What was going on? In November 1967 the *Western Mail* commissioned a survey to find out. It showed that three-fifths of voters in Wales now wanted Wales to have a Parliament, and the newspaper commented: 'After years of wandering in the Celtic twilight it is now possible that Wales and Scotland are poised to march into their own dawn.' Shortly afterwards the newspaper began to devote a lot of attention to the question of devolution. No newspaper in Britain, with the possible exception of *The Scotsman*, has given more attention to this important matter. It has seen to it that the issue has been fully reported and its implications thoroughly explored and analysed; indeed, the *Western Mail* has performed a notable service in the developing debate on devolution, one of the most important constitutional issues of the century. A year after the first survey, the newspaper commissioned another. This reinforced the findings of the first and confirmed the concern felt in Wales at the government's handling of Welsh problems. The paper nailed up its colours and called for a Welsh Parliament.

In 1968 Harold Wilson responded to the agitation in Wales and Scotland by ordering a Royal Commission to look into the question of home rule. The 1970 general election, however, seemed to many politicians to indicate that the nationalist tide was ebbing: Gwynfor Evans lost his seat and so did his counterpart in Scotland, Winifred Ewing. True, the Welsh nationalist party got almost an eighth of the Welsh vote, three times better than its 1966 performance, but it lost twenty-five deposits, now had no MP and was feeling bruised after failing to make much progress in local government elections that year.

Inside the Welsh Labour party there was a renewed struggle over the devolution issue. The majority of the party wanted a parliament or assembly, but some of the MPs thought it would encroach on their territory and depress their status; they thought that the office of Secretary of State would be undermined, and that Wales would be out of the mainstream of British politics. Nevertheless, other MPs agreed with the party view; they felt that devolution was right and necessary and that it would not destroy Labour's chances of winning a majority at Westminster. When the Royal Commission, now known as Kilbrandon, reported in 1973 it said that only a tenth of the Welsh people were happy with the existing way of running Welsh affairs; it recommended an elected legislative assembly for Wales, but not full self-government, saying that overriding control would be in the hands of the Westminster Parliament. 'Government seems to have been taken away from the people by its own sheer size and complexity,' the report said, 'leaving them with an uneasy impression that their feelings as individuals are no longer properly taken into account.'

Hopes that the nationalist tide has ebbed out of sight were rudely upturned by the elections of 1974. In February seven Scottish nationalist MPs were elected, and *Plaid Cymru* won in Merioneth and Caernarfon, losing Carmarthen by three votes. The new Welsh nationalist MPs, Dafydd Elis Thomas and Dafydd Wigley, were part of the younger generation of *Plaid Cymru* which was building a political organization on to the idealism of the pioneers. This generation was giving the party a more professional and more substantial look, knowing that voters wanted to hear about policies, that dreams must have nuts and bolts. Nationalist philosophy was being developed and given the muscles of well-researched economic, social and industrial plans. In the October election Gwynfor Evans got back into parliament, but *Plaid Cymru* still failed to make much progress in Labour's valley strongholds. Out of thirty-six seats fought, the party lost twenty-six deposits and it was broke. The unevenness of the party's support showed that there was still a long way to go; it was strong in rural Wales, from where it derived most of its money, but finding it hard going in most of the valleys.

Somehow it had to find a way of retaining its special appeal in the Welsh countryside and the towns of the north-west, keeping to its commitment to the language, while, at the same time, making its mark among the largely non-Welsh-speaking electorate in south Wales. Later there were signs that *Plaid Cymru* was slowly achieving this: the party began to win more seats on local authorities, and a survey showed that about half the party membership was not Welsh-speaking.

The success of the Scottish National party in the 1974 elections, and the recognition that offshore oil largely finished the argument that Scotland could not afford to be self-governing, put Scotland in the foreground in the devolution debate, and Wales had to ride the bubbles of Scotland's wake. It is a mistake to think that Welsh and Scottish nationalism are two halves of one creature, and there are significant differences between *Plaid Cymru* and the SNP. They spring from different backgrounds, have differences in outlook, ambition and composition, are not interdependent and are cousins rather than brothers. They both took roots in the twenties as small groups of writers, teachers and students; they were movements interested in the defence of national identities, but *Plaid Cymru* took the view that the language was at the heart of Welsh identity, while the SNP felt there was a strong Scottish identity based in the long-established institutions, the separate legal system and the relatively recent fact of nationhood. Scotland has been joined to England for a shorter time, since 1707, while Wales has been in harness at least since 1536 and is, of course, much closer to England. The profiles of the modern nationalist parties show important differences. *Plaid Cymru* has a strong cultural base, while the SNP has a strong economic base, a somewhat sharper business edge and a larger middle-class element. Carrying less weight in the Westminster Parliament, *Plaid Cymru* is not so assertive, but in some ways is more mature and sophisticated than the SNP, and certainly has more detailed and coherent policies.

After the general election of October 1974, John Morris, Secretary of State for Wales, was able to pursue his ambition to establish a Welsh Development Agency, a body with enough money, ideas and room to manoeuvre to attack the substantial economic difficulties of Wales. Fifty years of regional policies, a carrot here and a stick there, had helped Wales, but not enough; and the country remained vulnerable and underdeveloped. The idea of a large agency working to a coherent plan, and with more than a dash of entrepreneurial spirit, was broadly welcomed. Both the Confederation of British Industry and the new voice of Welsh trade unionism, the Wales TUC, supported it; the agency's job would be to promote industrial development, provide investment capital, take on responsibility for clearing derelict land. Meanwhile, in 1975, the powers of the Department of Trade and Industry in Wales were transferred to the Welsh Office, the largest devolutionary step since the Welsh Office itself was established.

That summer the Welsh Labour party and the Wales TUC renewed their commitment to the concept of an elected assembly, and the Conservative party restated its opposition, fearing that the assembly would be an expensive talking-shop, and a powerless one at that, and would lead to the breaking up of the United Kingdom.

The next step was for the government to make decisions on the machinery of the assembly and the kind of powers it should have. The debate began to gather momentum with the publication of the White Paper on devolution in November 1975 which set out the government's plans for assemblies in Edinburgh and Cardiff. It was the launch-pad for a great constitutional change, a political revolution. Only the most starry-eyed imagined that such an assembly in Cardiff would solve the difficulties of Wales with ease. The responsibility for its success would lie with the Welsh people. But it would offer the opportunity for improvement, for the better management of Wales, for the settlement of Welsh problems by Welsh people.

CHAPTER SEVEN

Flowers in the Meadow

The atmosphere of the Welsh countryside, magic and magnetic, has always drawn a trickle of city dwellers from their desks, benches and semi-detached homes, inviting them to settle in the hills and seek what promises to be a simpler and more fulfilling life, the craftsman's life or the smallholder's life, or a mixture of the two. In the past few years that trickle has become a considerable flow; and the hills of Wales ring to new sounds as the small army of immigrant craftsmen resettle districts made empty by the decline of the native society. Some are Welshmen returning to their old roots, doing what they had promised they would do as they jostled to the Underground or struggled once more into the breech of their dark business suits. But most are Englishmen, entranced by Wales, hoping to secure new roots and hoping for the kind of tranquillity they could never find in the cities.

Of course, a few of them retreat after a while and head back to the familiar pavements and traffic, their hopes cracked by money troubles or red tape, by their failure to integrate into another culture, another community, or sometimes by their own incompetence and laziness. The road from urban frustration to rural fulfilment is often a hard one and paved with rude awakenings.

The newcomers have bought up huts, cottages, farmhouses, farm buildings and mills. They have restored them and set to work as weavers, leather workers, jewellers, potters, garment makers, furniture builders, silversmiths, carvers, ironworkers, slate workers, toy makers and perfumers. They are former teachers, lawyers, civil servants, engineers, businessmen; all doing, in the modern phrase, their thing. Unlike many native craftsmen, who shape things in clay, metal and wood and cloth because their fathers and grandfathers were craftsmen before them, and who exist because there has always been a local need for their products, the new craftsmen come to craftsmanship from another direction, out of a dissatisfaction with their former lives and a new appreciation of the pleasures and rewards of working with their hands. They hope to stimulate, as well as satisfy, a demand for what they make. And in this age of mass production and uniformity they help to meet a growing appetite for hand-wrought goods, stuff with men's fingerprints upon it.

A number of newcomers have integrated into local communities, overcoming initial reservations, and have learned to get on in Welsh and have bilingual children who enjoy the education offered by small village schools. They have awareness and concern. 'I think we have a duty to learn Welsh,' a settler said. 'It is no good being at one with the countryside, being self-sufficient and doing a rewarding non-polluting job with your hands, while sticking out like a sore thumb in the cultural sense. Integration, in every way, is what it's all about.'

The new craftsmen, both Welsh and English, are helping to keep life in the hills. And in those areas that have always lost some of their brightest young people because of the lack of opportunities, the newcomers help to supply a necessary commercial outlook. Many of them are conservation-minded, able to look at the countryside and the threats, with new eyes. A man who has made a success of his weaving business in north Wales told me that he was leaving a large meadow by his mill untouched and ungrazed so that wild flowers would grow there. 'How many people today have seen meadows full of flowers? For most of us it is a rare sight or only a childhood memory. I want the flowers to grow in my meadow so that visitors can enjoy them.'

The simple life is not always as simple as it appears. I met a young man who was determined to be self-sufficient on his small patch of land. 'But you have to work a slave's hours,' he remarked, 'and money is always a worry. At the moment I'm trying to pluck up the courage to kill one of my pigs. If I am to see this thing through, if we are to eat, then it is right that I should kill a pig, but it may take me some time to steel myself to it.'

In some areas newcomers have earned a bad name as drifters and drop-outs. But the mere drop-out is usually the first to drop back to England. It is not only the hard work that deters him; his tranquil cottage may have no water supply or electricity, it often rains, and local authorities can be rather less than co-operative because they prefer people to live close to villages and not out in the hills where it is more difficult to provide services. The Council for Small Industries in Rural Areas is one of the organizations which helps people who want to set up workshops and says that the first thing a new settler must do is to win the confidence of his bank manager. 'There are many problems for the newcomers, but usually they are creative and sensitive people and are unlikely to damage the Welshness of the countryside. They want to be absorbed and have no wish to impose because Wales means something to them; and they are quite good at surviving. As our job is to help fight depopulation we are naturally pleased to see people like this.'

The standard of work among the craftsmen has been improving steadily and there are a number of bodies, like the Wales Tourist Board and the Design Council, encouraging better design and workmanship. The tourist board has been running a campaign to give Wales a better name for craftwork and souvenirs, and has been heavily critical of Welsh-flavoured knick-knacks, wrought in plastic and imported from the Far East. The craftsmen themselves have formed an association, the Welsh Crafts Trade Association, to improve standards and marketing, and quality, as well as quantity, is improving.

Judith Hoad, secretary of the association, and her husband Jeremiah, came from Canterbury to settle in Carmarthenshire, and had some desperate times before hitting on the idea of drawing postcards of Welsh scenes. They doubled their turnover each year. Their remote home on a hillside has no electricity and in the evenings the children sit as their parents read to them by the light of oil lamps. The Hoads say – and their remarks are echoed by many other newcomers – that they got out of the urban life because they found it dehumanizing. 'We have found a way of living that suits us better. When we left England people told us we were jumping into a wilderness and that we would soon be back. The truth is that we have jumped into a richer existence. We'll admit that it has been harder than we imagined, but all the more rewarding for that. We have learned to speak Welsh and our three children are bilingual. We believe that immigrants should go more than half-way to meet local people and become a part of the local scene. It is important to contribute to local life and defend it and not stand outside it.'

CHAPTER EIGHT

Reporting Wales

In common with most crafts and professions, journalism has a public image that, while not wholly false, is only true in patches. In films and television dramas and novels, journalists nearly always seem to emerge as rather unscrupulous and unsavoury characters, hallmarked by cirrhosis and halitosis, cynicism and dandruff. When I am introduced to people as a newspaperman I can see that they had expected a cross between a door-to-door salesman on a bad day and Humphrey Bogart in one of his nasty, five o'clock shadow roles, a B-picture man in a trench coat and trilby, a cigarette in the corner of his mouth, a hip flask maybe, and a voice processed into coke by cigarettes and shouting down telephones: hold the front page! But I am a disappointment. I have no cigarette wiggling on my lip edge, no trilby or flask, and I have never said, or heard anyone say: hold the front page! because every journalist knows that to try to hold the front page would be like trying to postpone sunset. Indeed, many journalists fail to live up (or down) to the image; they would not sell their grandmothers to make a story, they do some routine and useful work, sometimes important work, and they are kind to animals and children and even clean their shoes.

In spite of this prosaic reality, many of the people I meet in Wales still have a considerable interest in the work of reporters. Partly, they are curious to see themselves as others see them. Sometimes, people ask me to justify and explain the work I do. They ask: how does an Englishman, who does not have the Welsh language, report Welsh affairs for a national newspaper like *The Times*? It is not easy to provide a brief or complete answer. It is partly a matter of reporting technique and partly a matter of my own attitude to the task, and therefore, to some extent, of my own personality. When *The Times* invited me to go to Wales in the last month of 1968, their brief was a simple one: report Wales, communicate the significant news happenings, reflect the aspirations of the people, chart the changes and trends in Welsh life and opinion; report these, bearing in mind that *The Times* is a national newspaper and an international newspaper, read largely by people who may have only a superficial knowledge of the small country of Wales.

I had to be, in essentials, a foreign correspondent. And this is not at all facetious. From the beginning I have seen Wales as a country with a sense of its own traditions and identity. It has its own history, a different social and industrial development, special aspirations and problems. I keep these in my mind when I am writing. Like any foreign correspondent I have to put news events into their political, cultural and historical context, thinking in terms of the broad picture, always assuming that the reader is highly intelligent, but never assuming that he has detailed knowledge of Wales. The aim is to enable people in London, or Edinburgh, Southampton or Brussels to comprehend at once, to be able to pick up the threads.

So it is important for me to be aware of English attitudes to Wales and the position that Wales occupies in the United Kingdom and in Europe. If you ask how an Englishman reports Welsh affairs, he does it in much the same way, and for much the same reasons, that Americans, not Britons, report Britain to America. I am not saying that a Welshman born-and-bred, and a Welsh-speaker into the bargain, could not do the job magnificently, or better. Inevitably, though, he would look at Wales in a different fashion.

I always try to recall, when I am shaping and writing a report or article to be telephoned to London, what it felt like to be a stranger in Wales: largely ignorant, curious, awed. I remember thinking, as I sat in my first Welsh pub, contemplating my first half pint of Welsh bitter, that I could not pronounce the name on the inn sign or many of the telephone exchange names posted up in the call box. In the first few days, as I cut warily through the undergrowth, into deeper jungle, I began to appreciate something of the

complexity of Wales and wondered how I was going to grasp
it and sort it. I knew hardly anything of the country, of its
great events, big men, worries and tender spots. I had the
usual English notion of Wales, a hazy amalgam of coal,
black landscape, rugby footballers, choirs and hills (for
keeping a welcome in); but I was aware, in a professional
way, of the danger of taking preconceptions to a new place
and new situation. There seemed to be so much to learn that
Wales loomed in my consciousness as large as Australia. I
decided to keep my head down and listen, retain as open a
mind as possible, and try to view events through bifocals,
one half English, the other half Welsh. Many reporters
spend much of their time asking questions and not really
hearing the answers. But I have always tried to be as much a
listening journalist as a questioning one, because I believe
that at least half of journalism, half the satisfying of curiosity, is listening and watching. I also bought a yard of
books and began to listen to Wales talking. That was, and is,
rewarding because one of the best things about Wales is that
people like talking about the many facets of Welsh life, and
I have been fortunate in that my work enables me to travel
constantly throughout Wales, to talk to people at all levels
and of all views in a great variety of situations. I have also
had a grandstand view of numerous events, large and
small, of conflicts, follies and miseries as well as triumphs,
and I count myself fortunate that I have seen more of the
land of Wales than many Welshmen.

In spite of this growing familiarity, I have tried to keep a
part of me a stranger to Wales, to remain as far as is possible
a professional visitor, because detachment is a central ingredient of the kind of reporting I am involved in. There are
temptations, of course; the natural human temptation to
write kindly simply because all people like to be liked, and to
write kindly would make life more agreeable. That temptation has always to be resisted – and so has another temptation
which we journalists sometimes fall into, the temptation to
write unkindly simply to prove that one is nobody's man.
Or that one is smart. Both temptations can lead to a dis-
tortion of the truth, the first to a minimizing of the unpalatable,
the second to a maximizing of the unimportant. If journalists

have to be fair to those to whom they do not wish to be
fair, they must not, on the other hand, be unfair to those
to whom they would wish to be fair. And unfairness, from
whatever it springs, is bad journalism. Newspapermen
exist to disclose quickly, unlike academics; to expose,
to analyse critically and, where necessary, to attack or
deflate; but that is not the whole of journalism and there
should be room for the encouragement and recognition of
worth. Objectivity is one of journalism's fundamental parts
but is sometimes difficult to achieve because the truth
is not always an absolute. Facts are frequently obscured
or disputed and the truth becomes translated into the
interpretation that different individuals and groups place
upon the facts. Matters of fact are sometimes difficult
enough to report; when it comes to matters of belief,
strongly held and perhaps mistaken or distorted, the reporter begins his walk through the minefield.

As I remarked, the attitude of the foreign correspondent
seems to me the best approach for reporting the developing
story of Wales and the pieces of news and background that
go to make up the mosaic. Some knowledge of the history of
the country is therefore essential: it is not possible to write
properly without an historical perspective and in my kind of
journalism it is often necessary to trace a story to its roots
and hope that the reader will be interested enough to follow
the process. I do not think, for example, that it would be
possible to keep up a running commentary on the Welsh
language issue without knowing something of the language's
origins, of the effect of the Act of Union of 1536, of the
translation of the bible, of the 1870 Education Act, of Saunders Lewis's radio lecture of 1962. I do not think I could
write properly about coal mining if I did not know something of the geology of south Wales, if I did not visit coal
faces occasionally and speak to miners and managers. It
would be difficult to appreciate miners' problems and their
attitudes if I did not understand how mining developed in
the nineteenth century, how the miners' federation was
formed, what Mabon did, what happened in 1926. The
same applies to the steel industry and farming and the
post-war economic development of Wales, and the social

consequences of development. I would be in difficulty if I had no knowledge of the development of Welsh and Anglo-Welsh writing. It is one of the pleasures of this kind of specialized general reporting that each facet of Welsh life needs, and repays, careful exploration. One of the rewards of reporting Wales is that it has given me a complete education in a many-sided subject. Wales may be just a patch on the planet, but a man has to do a lot of driving, riding, walking, talking, listening and reading to know it well. And in many ways it is not small, not small in the parish pump sense. It is a microcosm and if it can be understood it can give you an insight into the issues and difficulties facing people throughout the world. My necessary education in the problems of the Welsh economy has enabled me to have a better understanding of the British economy and world economics; through coal miners and their families I have learned much about industrial communities and how they think, and why they think as they do; through my observations of Welsh politics I have learned much more about the way that people manage their affairs, how they scheme for power and exercise it; through my reporting of the language issue I have learned a lot about the way that people everywhere are concerned with matters like identity, community and survival. To know Wales is to be enriched. People say to me that Wales is claustrophobic, a backwater that can teach nothing of value, that its history and culture are a waste of time; I think, rather, it is they who are myopic. Wales can be a good window on the world, a place of reasonable and comprehensible human scale from which it is possible to see and understand and measure much of what goes on in the world. It is a root. There is no need for people to choose between Wales and 'the wide world' – whatever they mean by that – because they can have both, in their schools, in their social lives, in their pursuits.

If knowledge of the historical, industrial, geographical and social background is important, is it also important that a 'foreign correspondent' should know Welsh? It is a question I am often asked. Broadly speaking, it is not essential that the Welsh affairs correspondent of a Fleet Street newspaper should be able to speak Welsh and I have only occasionally felt disadvantaged in my reporting because I do not know the language well enough to speak it. On only one occasion have I been refused an interview on language grounds: a young man said to me, through a friend who interpreted, that he intended no disrespect or impoliteness, but he had no wish to be interviewed in English. I respected his point of view. I knew the background against which he made his point – and people do not have to give interviews if they do not want to. As it happened, his reasons for not giving an interview told me significantly more about the situation I was examining for an article, and therefore provided more information for readers. When I had been in Wales a short time I made a decision, based upon my instinct and early reading of the cultural situation at that time, that I would not learn Welsh, at least for some time. It was partly a matter of being practical – having worked hard as an adult to gain a good command of French I knew that learning a language requires a lot of time and patient study, and I did not want to waste time in a desultory attempt to learn Welsh. I would want to do it properly or not at all. It was also a matter of being impartial, of being a professional onlooker. In the late nineteen-sixties and early seventies the Welsh language issue, on which I was writing a continuous report, was a very hot one. To have thrown myself into learning the language then might have involved an emotional commitment that might have coloured my reporting. I was not prepared to take the risk. I think it is probably a mistake for a reporter to try to go completely native in any situation, and as a natural non-joiner I felt there were dangers in entering a particular fold. Today, however, much of the emotion and anger have vaporized and the language question can be debated more reasonably, although it certainly has not disappeared. I find that after more than six years of contact with Welsh I have absorbed, more or less passively, a small collection of nouns, a few verbs, adjectives and pleasantries, because I have a natural interest in words and languages. I can read a little and understand a little, and I feel that to know the language better, just for its own sake, would enable me to enjoy Wales more fully and to understand it better. I would like to be able to read newspapers and periodicals in Welsh. If only one could be given a language through a hypodermic.

A large measure of detachment is important in reporting as a safeguard of fairness and balance. One has to be cool, but not cold because there has to be warmth and compassion, too. But remaining a newcomer becomes progressively more difficult for a reporter as time passes. I try to keep my professional mind fresh and hold myself to my rule that anything new to me should be reported; and, of course, many of the subjects on which I have written need to be looked at again, to be revised, reworked and re-presented in the light of new information and changing circumstances. The constant sharpening of the sense of curiosity, of nosiness and concern, is of the essence. I count myself fortunate to be doing this kind of reporting because it is a mixture of hard news, interpretative writing and feature-writing, general yet specialized. There is also room to write pieces which are entertaining as well as informative. The work gives me the kind of independence in which I originate most of my own material and take most of the decisions, in consultation with my news desk in London, on what I should write about. Few journalists in Britain have an opportunity to do this kind of work because British journalism does not have much room for it; and that, I think, is a deficiency.

The people of the British Isles know little of each other. On the whole they are ignorant of their own still-united kingdom and its component parts. There are several reasons for this and one of them is that the national press has failed them, and continues to fail them, in the matter of telling them what is going on in the countries and regions of Britain. To some extent the broadcasters in radio and television have a part in this failure. Much of the national press and other sections of the communications business are centralist, self-centred and hidebound. Old-fashioned in terms of machinery, production techniques and manning, much of the press is also old-fashioned in the attitudes it has to life outside the walls of Westminster, the City and EC4. The people who direct the gathering of news, and many of the people who write it, are usually content, when they look at Wales, Scotland, the west and the north, to plough a well-

worn furrow of stereotype and cliché. Many have grown too
lazy to lift the stones and reporters sometimes do not go out
to find out about a particular situation, but instead go out
to shape something to an idea preconceived in the office.
New recruits, even though many of them come from the
regions, get drawn into the conventions, the myths and the
set attitudes of the industry. A lot of them simply slice
off their roots and, in the process, give up one of the
journalist's essential pieces of equipment, his sense of
curiosity.

Now this is a broad sweep of criticism and it is true that
there are exceptions and instances that can be cited in miti-
gation, but I do not think they affect the substance of my
criticism.

The popular press in this country developed as education
was making the mass of the people literate. The newspapers
naturally reflected the age, the pride in empire and the sense
of superiority of Britishness, a concept in which Wales and
Scotland joined, not unanimously but certainly overwhelmingly. Welshness and Scottishness were kept under hatches
and were well-regulated. The press, like government, like all
the great institutions of culture, commerce and public
affairs, was rooted firmly in London, the centre of one of
the most centralized states in Europe. The sense of metro-
politan superiority and its undercurrent of anti-provincialism pervaded the vital areas of politics, the civil service,
the institutions, the arts and the press. Local newspapers
were founded to meet purely local needs and, occasionally,
papers were started, like the *Manchester Guardian*, *The
Scotsman* and the *Western Mail*, which expressed a regional
identity, but generally there was not much to challenge
London's superiority. It was the hive where the honey was
and accrued most of the talent, and still is and still does. The
provinces were made to feel second-class and unsmart.
When Wilfred Pickles read the news on the BBC there were
scandalized cries at his Yorkshire accent (though most of
the complaints came from Yorkshiremen). In Wales there
was not only an accent but another language that Englishmen found unpronounceable and hilarious. The London attitude, the British attitude, to Wales prevailed and it was

part of a climate in which people sought to gravitate to the centre. Meanwhile, the education system largely ignored the history, geography and social and industrial development of the regions of Britain. During my own schooling in England the subjects of Wales, Scotland and Ireland were covered in minutes, but I spent much time learning about the beastly Boers. It is an unfortunate effect of the way that education and journalism have developed in the past century that we know so little of each other. The British people have had to rely on caricatures. The national press, the broadcasting systems and much of the provincial press, which should all reflect life in Britain as it really is, tend to take the London view, founded in stereotypes and myth; and that is a distorted view.

Perhaps it is time for a kind of foreign reporting within the British Isles. It is time that the Fleet Street newspapers reviewed their attitudes to the parish that lies north of Watford and west of the Hammersmith flyover. The bitter situation in northern Ireland came as a great surprise to most of the people of mainland Britain: newspapers hardly ever bothered to examine the rising tensions and social conditions in Ulster before the tinder was ignited in 1969. The rise of nationalism in Scotland and Wales came as a great surprise to the uninformed English because the bulk of the national press and the regional press in England had either ignored it or laughed at it, though mainly ignored it. Regional assemblies are going to be established in Cardiff and Edinburgh and the majority of the English people will not know how or why an event of enormous constitutional importance came about, because their newspapers have not told them. We do not understand our neighbours and that makes it more difficult for us to have an insight into the problems and attitudes of people in the United Kingdom, in Europe and further afield. Internationalism, much talked of, must surely begin at home; the patchy and silly reporting of regional and foreign affairs by much of the British press has contributed to English insularity.

It is true that regional caricatures have their place and that leg-pulling about our differences is one of the lubricants that makes life easier. But what has happened in the newspaper world is that regional caricatures have too often become accepted as the reality.

I suppose that this can make life easier for a reporter dispatched from London to cover a regional story, but there is often a gap between the image and the reality. Some years ago I was among journalists who covered a serious pit accident in south Wales in which several men were killed. After we had been to the pit head for information we went to a nearby inn to write and telephone reports and await developments. After a while, a group of breathless reporters, fresh from those Fleet Street papers which did not have staff reporters in Wales, came in. They were perplexed. They had just been to the pit and they wanted to know why there was no group of weeping women there, dressed in shawls and cradling babies. Things had changed in the last three-quarters of a century, but they, having been sent to write about a harrowing scene that was fixed firmly in their minds, felt nonplussed.

In die-stamp popular journalism much news is moulded to conventions. All newspapers have to be commercial packages and the commercial nature of them is strongly in the minds of the men and women who make the decisions on selection and treatment of the news material that comes into their offices. The way that spot news is handled is usually very good and fits the expectations of habitual readers. But analysis tends to be weaker. After the top serious news, the accent in popular newspapers is on short and bright stories and trivia – for sound commercial reasons. In the final news mix a funny Welsh story has a better chance of getting into the paper than a serious Welsh story, particularly if it fits a stereotype. And although Fleet Street newspapers claim to be national papers preference is given to news that happens in London and the home counties, because that is where the circulation is highest. The matter is further compounded by the practice of editionizing. This means that regional stories published in the first editions of morning newspapers tend to be cut out and replaced by London-rooted stories in later editions. The early editions have to catch the trains to the colonies; the later editions circulate only in London. So that when regional stories are published they tend to be read mainly in the regions. Again, there are commercial reasons for this, but the practice is a negation of what national newspapers should be doing. The serious and continuous commentary on what is happening in the regions is made by only two or three papers. The popular press concerns itself essentially with the news of the day in the regions – murders, accidents, feuds, strikes and runaway vicars – and pieces of commentary and explanation of regional affairs are rare. In any case they tend to be done by visiting writers (who, when they come to Wales find it difficult not to adopt a Duw-indeed-to-goodness style, which comes from reading too many pre-war novels about south Wales) and it means that people in the regions get from London papers only the stage-image of themselves, and they have even come to believe it themselves. When I went to Scotland to do research for an article, a Scottish journalist said: 'I hope you're not going to do a typical Fleet Street job: Scotland in twenty-four hours and och in every other line.'

Headlines are even more hackneyed in most national and provincial papers. Scotland is encapsulated, as the journalist suggested, by Och and Hoots Mon; Wales by Look You; Ireland by Begorrah; the north by By Gum. Newspapers package women as well as regions, and some reference to hair colour and bosom size is almost obligatory. The defence may be that newspapers are only giving readers what they want, but circulations are falling and newspapers ought, perhaps, to consider more carefully the sort of information service they provide, within a commercial framework. Among some of the people who decide what goes into our newspapers, in Fleet Street and in the provinces, there is a dreadful attitude made of outdated views, philistinism, centralism and ignorance.

The problem of under-reporting exists in television, too. A television news programme has to cover an enormous range of events in twenty minutes or half an hour and it, too, has to have an element of entertainment, has to be a news mix, with decisions taken on priorities, bearing in mind the availability of film. Television and radio are unrivalled for immediacy and drama and no newspaper could hope to compete with some of the things that television does. The evening news is often the front page of the next morning's papers, and television is best when it is involved in incident journalism – the ship on the rocks, the war, the major accident, the face-to-face interviews with the principals in important and dramatic situations. But television news programmes can really spare little time for the explanation of issues, in the regions or elsewhere, and often they are not very good at reporting the issues from which incidents derive. Television often fails to inform clearly and sometimes serves only to bewilder. We see pictures of marching strikers and angry men shouting into the microphone, but there seems to be little time for the item to be fitted into a context. We see people evicted from a house and we can see that they are in tears, but we are left unable to grasp the housing problems in their district or how they got into a mess. We see language demonstrators struggling with policemen, but we learn little of the language issue in Wales. Because we do not derive understanding from a series of news fragments, we need longer television news programmes, as we now have on radio, and probably fewer items. Only in that way will television journalists, who often have a difficult enough task, be able to do justice to themselves, to the people they interview, to the situations they report – and sometimes affect – and to the viewer. Radio, which has more room and more flexibility, is better suited to the exploration of some issues – and the BBC recently took up the idea of foreign reporting within Britain with the programme *In Britain Now*.

Inside Wales, television and radio have helped the Welsh people to identify more closely with Wales and with each other, have helped to increase national consciousness. The only daily newspaper published in Wales, the *Western Mail*, which has a circulation of about one hundred thousand, has also contributed to this awareness and sense of entity; although in north Wales its circulation is weak and this area is served primarily by the Liverpool *Daily Post*. The BBC and HTV, the commercial company, have none of the economic and distribution problems of newspapers, and their news programmes start on the assumption that Wales is an entity, so that south Welshmen and north Welshmen get a regular look at each other, and each other's problems.

The acceptance of the principle of separate broadcasting for Wales, and the founding of the Welsh Home Service in 1937, were important steps in Welsh life, far-reaching in their effects. They opened the way to Wales-based broadcasting journalism and the development of broadcasting journalism in the Welsh language. Because the opportunities for young men and women to practise journalism in Welsh are restricted – there is only one national weekly paper, *Y Cymro*, which has openings for trainees – the BBC and HTV have large responsibilities in this field. As radio and television reporting in Wales grows, in both English and Welsh, the demand for highly-trained and critical journalists will have to be met. The establishment of a Welsh assembly will make new demands on the reporting services. For the Welsh-language news services the problem of recruiting staff of the right calibre is already acute: there are not enough Welsh-speaking people entering journalism, and the implications are serious. If anyone contemplating a career in reporting has reservations because of the ruffian image of newspapermen, I would say that even in my own time journalism has become, at its sharp end, a little more gentlemanly. When I started working for a local newspaper I was sent to write about the romance of a fish and chip shop proprietor's daughter who had eloped. I soon found myself in the company of a body of men from Fleet Street. The fish and chip shop proprietor, however, said he would give an interview to only one reporter and we were to choose. We went to an inn to parley, but two old hands could not agree. So they stripped to the waist and there in that bar they wrestled for the right to hear the frier's tale. Today, it would not happen, I think. If it did, though, the combatants would at least keep their shirts on.

Cymruology has not confined me to the eight thousand square miles of Wales. The pursuit of Welsh, and related matters has taken me to Brittany, Ireland, Scotland and the United States as well as to almost every village and valley from Sully Island to the South Stack, from Point of Air to St David's Head. Once I was part of a Boeingful of Welsh people – businessmen, industrialists, craftsmen, singers and sellers – who flew to stage a trade fair in New York, earn some dollars through business forays and generally bang a drum for Wales in the most ambitious effort ever made to sell Wales in America. The Morriston Orpheus choir, from Swansea, went along to help charm the Americans into submission with their marvellous sound.

The forerunners of this Welsh expedition, in the last century and before, had lived on prayer and hard tack as they had crossed the Atlantic. But this raiding party crossed in very different style, with the choir and supporters in full flight of song, and the captain and two of the cabin staff making their announcements in Welsh. Probably it was the first Welsh-language transatlantic flight, and, after a while, the whole thing resembled a bank holiday charabanc outing to Porthcawl. The stern Welshmen of long ago, who pioneered America in the wagon – and on the wagon – would have turned in their graves to hear the air hostess say: '*Does dim rhagor o gwrw*' ('There's no more beer'), and see the shudder that ran through the aircraft.

It is hard for a very small country to make an impact on a very large one and, in New York, the city that dwarfs, the roar of the red dragon sounded a little like the roar of a mouse. But there are important economic links between Wales and America, as well as historical ones: American investment in Wales is worth more than three hundred and fifty million pounds, and more Welsh people work in the one hundred and four American-owned factories in Wales than work in the coal industry.

The Welsh expedition coincided with the annual North American *gymanfa ganu*, or singing festival, an occasion where two thousand Americans with Welsh blood in their veins assemble to moisten their thinning roots and to sing fairly badly the hymns of long ago. From the balcony of the New York Hilton ballroom I looked down at them: a cottonfield of white heads and hardly a young voice among them.

A fake Welsh inn had been erected inside the hotel, a poor plastic thing, the like of which had never been seen in Wales. When it was opened everyone had a free pint, but, quite soon, the barman, who spoke Brooklyn, not Welsh, shouted: 'All drinks from now on are one dollar fifty!' The effect was instant. Before you could say *iechyd da* the Welsh turned and fled, like a herd of bison that had just seen Buffalo Bill unsheath his Winchester 73.

There are still some vestiges of the Dylan Thomas industry in the United States. New York was, of course, Dylan's death-place and, one evening, a group of us were invited to go to P. J. Clarke's, a bar where the poet had been an habitué. We went as pilgrims to a shrine and drank and talked for a little while until our pilgrimage was interrupted by the arrival of an American gentleman we had met earlier, who was something big in vacuum cleaners. He was clutching to his breast a bottle of champagne and, such was his excitement at meeting us, so animated were his movements and his handshakes, that the cork blew out of the champagne bottle with a loud report and ricocheted from the ceiling. In a little less than a trice the barman ran around the counter to tell us angrily that we were now guilty of breaking the law in having an open bottle of liquor in his bar. And quite suddenly the light in our corner dimmed, as in an eclipse, as two or three very tall and very broad men with grim expressions and the sensitive charm of Sherman tanks, rose from their bar stools and spoke one word to the group of us.

'Out.'

There is a time to argue, and a time not to argue. Out under the stars in the warm street we reflected that to be thrown out of a Dylan Thomas shrine in such a fashion was piquant, to say the least. Certainly the poet himself would have enjoyed hugely the manner of our going.

Index